STORM W[ATER]
A JOURNE[Y]
TO
DISCIPLESHIP

JAMES N COOPER

STORM WATCH: A Journey To Discipleship

The Team:
Author: James N. Cooper
Copyright National Library of Congress 2015
Project Coordinator: James N. Cooper
Manuscript Editor: Sarah Serena
Cover Art Coordinator: Richard A. Kinkead

Reference Books and Articles:
The Holy Bible
King James Version
New Living Translation
New International Version
Merriam-Webster online dictionary
www.Wikipedia.org
News articles from the World Wide Web.
    2015 by James N Cooper
All rights reserved. This book may not be reproduced or used in any form without the written permission from the author.

Dedicated to my wife Jennifer. For being my strength and my hope when I had little of both. Without you, I wouldn't be the man I am today and for that, I thank you.

STORM WATCH: A Journey to Discipleship

Table of Contents:

Prologue
Introduction
Chapter 1 The Summer of 1994
Chapter 2 Fire Insurance
Chapter 3 Understanding What Sin is
Chapter 4 God has a Plan
Chapter 5 What is Heaven Like?
Chapter 6 We Have a Loving God
Chapter 7 Jesus Christ, My Savior
Chapter 8 Time Marches On
Chapter 9 Our New Beginning
Chapter 10 Cause for Alarm
Chapter 11 What about Hell?
Chapter 12 Storm Watch
Chapter 13 Trials and Tribulations
Chapter 14 Only God Knows
Chapter 15 Awake
Chapter 16 Broken
Chapter 17 Time to Heal
Chapter 18 Thank God for Prayer and Family
Chapter 19 Back to Columbus? No Thank you
Chapter 20 Clock. Cup. Rug.
Chapter 21 Raw Snorgs
Chapter 22 Today is the Best Day of My Life
Chapter 23 One Last Ride
Chapter 24 War of the Worlds
Chapter 25 A Lesson from Hesson
Chapter 26 Soldier of Misfortune
Chapter 27 Doing God's Will

Chapter 28 Get Right or Get Left
Chapter 29 Do Not Be a Charlatan
Chapter 30 Listening to God
Chapter 31 Peace after the Storm

"Blessed is the one who perseveres under trial because, having stood the test, that person will receive the crown of life that the Lord has promised to those who love him." James 1:12 (NIV)

Introduction
Sometimes Nice Guys Finish Last

I consider myself for the most part, a nice guy. A good guy. Someone that you can depend on when the going gets tough. After all, I don't party, cheat, or "raise a ruckus" like so many others, and I've never made the news for some awful crime. I've always thought of myself as an Average Joe; a simple man. I'm a hard worker, and I value my family time. Like many, I just want to live the American dream. I've always tried living this dream by the golden rule, do unto others….

There is a common belief among the masses, that being "the salt of the earth," will one day give them an all access ticket through the pearly gates of Heaven. Some might think if they put a little extra in the offering plate on Sunday morning, perhaps that will be enough to get them into the Promised Land? This unfounded conclusion couldn't be further from the truth. You cannot place your hopes in the inaccurate belief that if you are a good person, surely God will accept your goodness as payment for your transgressions.

The Bible teaches us that our best works are like filthy rags to God. *But we are all as an unclean thing, and all our righteousnesses are as filthy rags; and we all do fade as a leaf; and our iniquities, like the wind, have taken us away.* Isaiah 64:6. Good deeds are not enough to get you into

Heaven. While God is pleased with our good works, He will not accept our very best for a payment of sin. We could invest all our time and money in good deeds for humanity, but even that's not enough to cover our sins. We are all sinners in the eyes of the Lord. Since God is Holy and cannot look upon sin, there must be a replacement for our iniquities.

According to God's Word, there must be a replacement that God will accept. The great news is, there is such a substitute. His name is Jesus Christ. He came to this earth more than two thousand years ago to be our Redeemer. Faith in Jesus Christ is the only way to Heaven. God acknowledges the death, burial, and resurrection as atonement for our sins. This is the only payment God will accept. You cannot enter Heaven without believing in Jesus as your Deliverer. John 14:6 reads: *Jesus saith unto him, I am the way, the truth, and the life: no man cometh unto the Father, but by me.* Read on.

When I was young, I lived next door to my grandparents and spent a lot of time at their house. My grandparents raised eleven children and had twenty-one grandchildren. Truth be told, they raised most of the grandchildren too. Nine of the grandchildren lived only a few houses down, so they always had company. My grandparents had good "old fashioned" values, therefore I was raised up not to do drugs or alcohol. I knew that if I did, it would break their hearts. Their love was enough for me to never try that stuff. That's just how we were raised. As I grew up into adulthood, new and different temptations arose.

I'm not saying I was perfect. In fact I'm saying I was far from it. I had a good heart and I've always tried to do the right thing, yet there were times that I did fall into temptation. I was like any other kid growing up in the 80's, except I was missing one thing. I had great family and friends, but I lacked faith. I was the *good guy.* A good guy that despite myself, sinned on a daily basis. One day I had a thought I couldn't get out of my mind: If I die today, will I go to Heaven?

There have been several "good guys" who failed to make it into Heaven because they didn't know Jesus as their Savior. Ephesians 8:9 says, *For by grace are ye saved through faith; and that not of yourselves: [it is] the gift of God:* Many in today's society really believe that benevolence and kindness will get them to Heaven one day. This is a false belief and far from what the Bible teaches. Matthew 7:21-23 states: *Not every one that saith unto me, Lord, Lord, shall enter into the kingdom of heaven; but he that doeth the will of my Father which is in heaven. Many will say to me in that day, Lord, Lord, have we not prophesied in thy name? And in thy name have cast out devils? And in thy name done many wonderful works? And then will I profess unto them, I never knew you: depart from me, ye that work iniquity.* It is a fine thing to be nice to your brother, but don't base your eternal salvation on your good deeds. This belief is a false hope.

So how does one get to Heaven anyways? Well that part my friend is simple. It is a gift from God Almighty Himself. This gratuity is offered to every nation, race, and individual. God does however, give us a choice to accept this bounty of eternal happiness or decline it. The Bible teaches us in Romans 3:23 - *For all have sinned, and come short of the glory of God;* And Romans 6:23 - *For the wages of sin [is] death; but the gift of God [is] eternal life through Jesus Christ our Lord.* God makes it possible for every man to work out his salvation. It's up to you to choose your own path.

God provides us with only one way to make it into Heaven. We all qualify for this wonderful reward, but how does one acquire God's offer of eternal salvation? It's as easy as knowing you're A B C's: We must Accept, Believe, and Confess.

Accept: First you must accept that Jesus Christ is the Son of God, the Savior of the world, and follow Him. When you receive Jesus Christ as Lord and Savior, the Holy Spirit takes up residency in your heart, so you can have a personal relationship with our Savior. Jesus wants to have an innermost personal relationship with you.

Believe: Believe that He died on the cross for the sins of the world and rose again on the third day. Believing in the death, burial, and resurrection is an essential part of being a Christian. Jesus knew no sin yet He bore the sins of the world for you and me. Jesus defeated death, Hell, and the devil on the day that He rose again. The devil did his worst, but it clearly wasn't enough. Romans 10:9 says: *That if thou shalt confess with thy mouth the Lord Jesus, and shalt believe in thine heart that God hath raised him from the dead, thou shalt be saved.*

Confess: Lastly, confess your sins to God and ask Him for forgiveness. John 1:9 tells us: *If we confess our sins, he is faithful and just to forgive us our sins, and to cleanse us from all unrighteousness.* Jesus goes on to tell us in Revelation 3:19: *As many as I love, I rebuke and chasten: be zealous therefore, and repent.* You must confess your sins **and** repent of them. Confession is understanding the things that you've done wrong in the eyes of God, and admitting them to the Lord. Then you must repent of your sins. To repent means to turn away from your sin. It's a change of heart. Acts 2:38 tells us that once we know our ABC's: accept, believe, and confess, we will then receive the gift of the Holy Spirit, which dwells inside of the new believer. The Holy Spirit acts as a compass, guiding you along in your Christian journey.

God's path to righteousness seems elementary, yet so many people fall short of God's plan of redemption. I know now that it's every Christian's duty to share the Gospel; that's one reason why I'm writing this book. I hope it will reach the lives of many unsaved souls. I also want to reach out to the newly converted Christian, and to give them a glimpse of "what's next" in their personal walk with Jesus Christ. When I was a new believer, I didn't know how to grow as a Christian. It took many years for me to understand God's plan. Permit me to share an intimate story of how I became a Christian, my journey through discipleship, and how I almost became a statistic like so many other "good people."

1

The Summer of 1994

In the summer of 1994 I was a young man who just graduated from middle school, and I was trying to find my way in this world. Our middle school was small enough, with only around eighty children in attendance. I remember thinking, "I have the whole summer off before high school starts, but what should I do with it?" Entering high school was going to be a major change for me. I spent kindergarten through eighth grade with the same eighty kids. This was a brand new high school from a consolidation, which housed over two thousand students. I feared I would never see my friends again, and even if I do, things would most certainly be different.

A few weeks into summer break, I received a phone call from one of my friends inviting me to play in a basketball tournament. The competition would consist of kids our age from all around the tri state area. He told me that we would be competing in the summer championship series. Since basketball was my life back then, I gladly accepted. We spent many hours playing basketball in middle school, and everyone from the old team was going to be there. I couldn't wait for the day to arrive. I figured this might be the last time we all would get to play basketball together. My thinking was this: One last hoorah, and I wanted to go out with a bang.

The day quickly arrived and my mother dropped me off at my friend's house. I was a little early, so I started greeting some of the parents who were chatting in the driveway. We generally took two mini vans so everyone would have plenty of room. After the last guy arrived, it looked like we were ready to go. I asked, "Who will I be riding with?" My friend looked at me and smiled, "All of us. We are waiting for the church van to get here."

Church van? What was he talking about? A little irritated I said, "Now hold on a minute. What do you mean church van?" He started to explain himself. He said that the tournament is considered a church function, but not to worry. I had no idea what that meant. "I thought we were going to play basketball? Now we are heading to church? What gives?" I felt very uneasy when asking about the church function, because I didn't know what to expect for an answer. "Why are we riding in a church van anyways?" He explained himself a little more thoroughly this time. He said that I wouldn't have to act or do anything differently, and that the tournament was sponsored by several area churches.

After the initial shock set in, I had no problem that it was a church function. It's just, I've never really gone to church. Well, once I was invited to a pizza party at my uncle's church when I was six years old. A few of my cousins and I went to church and they had a puppet show for all the children. They passed out Bibles to those who didn't have one. That's all I really remember about church when I was a child. I only went once. I had pizza and saw Kermit the Frog. I had always been intrigued about going to church; my mom just never took me. There were times that I would ask questions when I was growing up like any kid would do such as, "Is there a God? Where is Heaven?" My mother would answer them to the best of her ability. That's about as far as the conversation usually went though.

My family was very different when it came to discussing religion. Now that I look back, it was because everyone had their own point of views on the subject, and it was just easier that way. I found out many years later that my grandmother was a Sunday school teacher when she was younger, but surprisingly never discussed faith. To her defense, it was the parent's responsibility to share the Gospel. We just didn't talk about it as a family.

I always paid close attention anytime the adults had a conversation about religion. From time to time a few out-of-the-way family members from up yonder, (what most would consider the country) would come by and speak to my grandparents about God. It was very interesting to me as a child to hear them discuss theology, but most of the time their debates would end in an argument about what the truth really is. This all sped through my mind like a rocket as I climbed into the van. I thought to myself that if all my friends are coming along too, what's the worst thing that could happen?

Once we arrived at the tournament, our team couldn't wait to play basketball. Looking around, I saw several games that were already in progress. The rules were simple. Teams would progress up in the bracket with a win and they are allowed two losses before elimination. I thought with our talent, we were sure to win, and win we did. Well.... for the first few games anyways.

Soon it was time for lunch, and I was starving. I worked up quite an appetite while playing some serious defense. I wondered what they would be serving for lunch. The aroma of pizza soon filled the arena as they rolled it in on delivery carts. Every young man loved pizza. I couldn't wait any longer, so I quickly started chowing down.

A man with a microphone started thanking everyone for coming to today's event. This man was dressed in a shirt and tie, and looked very important. He quickly got my attention when he did something that I will never forget. He said, "We will now bless the food." What? How do you do that? Even though I considered myself somewhat intelligent, I knew nothing when it came to "blessing the food." I looked around and everyone stopped what they were doing and bowed their heads. As he blessed the food, I stopped eating too and bowed my head out of respect. I'd never experienced someone praying before, especially thanking God for lunch.

Once the prayer was over, we began to eat again as the guy kept talking. Everyone was scarfing down pizza while listening earnestly to what the speaker had to say. There were a few trouble makers goofing off to the side of me, but I paid no attention to them. I was absorbing all of this new information in like a sponge.

I could tell that the man speaking was on a mission. He opened his Bible and began telling us about Jesus Christ. The pastor told us that Jesus died on an old rugged cross for everyone's sins, and He rose again on the third day. He is now seated at the right hand of the Father.

Jesus? The messenger explained that Jesus is the Son of God Almighty and He came to earth some 2000 years ago to die for everyone's sins. He explained that we are all sinners and have fallen short of the glory of God and without repentance, we all would go to a sinner's Hell.

Hell? Sinning? These were all things that I'd never been introduced to before. My mind was overwhelmed with all this new information. Those words were strong to hear and understand for the first time. Something deep inside told me that the words he spoke were true. As the orator finished speaking, he asked everyone to bow their heads, so I did. He asked everyone in the group a simple question, "Do you believe that Jesus Christ is the Son of God?" He then asked, "Do you believe that Jesus died on the cross for everyone's sins?"

The speaker made a plea to the unbeliever. "Those who believe what I say is true and believe it for the first time, please raise your hand." Since the pastor was reading from the Bible; I knew it had to be true, so I raised my hand. I didn't know much about faith but I knew that the Bible was the Word of God and anything in it must be true because it came from God. Many hands went up. He then asked, "Do you want to be saved from a sinner's Hell? If so, keep your hand up." I remember thinking, "What am I doing? Should I leave my hand up or put it down?" I believed in the things the man was speaking about." I took a leap of faith and kept my hand up. The man asked for everyone that wasn't saved, to repeat this prayer after him. "Dear Heavenly Father, I know I am a sinner....."

After the prayer was complete, the speaker said that if I prayed this prayer and meant it with all my heart, I was now saved and would go to Heaven someday. I didn't even know that I could go to Hell. It had never crossed my mind. I was very naïve when it came to these things. I thought that Hell was just reserved for murderers, prostitutes, and people that hated God. That's how Hollywood painted it on the big screen, and that's what I believed right up to this point. There's no way that I could ever hate God, and I wasn't a murderer. I just didn't *know* who God was. I was never introduced to Him before. I realized just then that I'd lived my whole life not knowing anything about Jesus. I remember trying to gather my thoughts of the events that just transpired. As I pulled myself together I thought, "Wow, I'm going to Heaven one day. Although the preacher's words were brief, they were also significant and worthwhile. It felt good to know that someone took the time to tell me about Jesus.

After everyone finished lunch, we continued playing basketball. Once our team lost the final game we made our way to the van. While on the way home, I pondered on that man's words and what they meant to me. I knew in my heart the words were real and true. I felt that I was blindsided by today's events, but I'm glad I went. I didn't wake up this morning expecting to be saved. If my teammates would have told me that there could be a slight chance that the Gospel would be shared, I might not have gone along for the journey.

2

Fire Insurance

It was a long ride home with everyone disheartened from our defeat. I knew this would be the last time our team would play together. I was hoping we would go out on top as winners. I could see the calamity on each and every one of their faces, and the defeat in their eyes, as I looked around the van. After a few moments, I remembered what transpired during halftime. I *was* a winner that day. I'm now saved. I felt a gladness come over me as I began to digest it all. Should I tell my friends about it? What would they think? They'd probably make fun of me, besides everyone still had that "Don't mess with me" demeanor. They were disheartened because our team lost the tournament. Is there something that I should do now that I am saved? Should I read the Bible? My gladness quickly turned to apprehension. I didn't know what the right answer was.

All these questions quickly flooded my mind. I wasn't sure if I could handle my new found faith. I didn't know how to be a Christian. As these thoughts barreled through my head, I started feeling uneasy. I now see that it was the devil filling my mind full of skepticism and doubt. From this point on, because I didn't know how to grow and have a personal relationship with Jesus, I chose to put my faith on the back burner. At least until I had a better understanding of it. By doing this, I shut God out. For the first time in my life, even though I thought I was saved, I felt distant and lost.

I quickly started using my recent transformation as a safety net when it came to discussing religion. Since I didn't know very much at all about my new found faith, I was a little apprehensive to discuss it with anyone. I found out that people in general didn't really want to confer over the Bible, they just wanted to know if I was saved. That was a good thing because I wouldn't have been able to tell them very much about the Bible or God. I was uneducated in that sense. If someone asked me, "Are you saved?" I would simply say, "Yeah, sure am. I was saved at a basketball camp during a lunch break. It was fantastic."

I hate to say it, but that seemed to be enough to get people off my back at the time. This would soon be my scapegoat for anything religious that would come my way. After all, the preacher at the basketball event said that I must believe in Jesus. He told me to make it to Heaven you must believe. I believed....so I'm good, right? I totally missed the fact that I needed to grow in character and know God on a personal level. I looked at God as the Creator of the universe. How could I ever approach Him? I had no idea at the time.

I was blinded by the fact that I could have an interconnection with Jesus Christ. The devil did his best to keep me from the knowledge of Christ. That day, the preacher didn't give me instructions on how to grow as a Christian. He didn't tell me that I should read the Bible, pray, and speak to God. Looking back, I know that I did believe in my heart that Jesus was the Son of God. I repented of my sins, but I did not follow Jesus. I did not know how to. I'm not blaming the preacher at the camp for not instructing me on the next steps in my Christian journey; after all he did more for me than anyone else. He shared the truth and the Gospel. He introduced me to my Savior Jesus Christ.

Was the man in Matthew 8:21-22, me? In the Book of Matthew, the Bible informs us that one of Jesus's disciples wanted to follow Him; but only when it was more convenient for him to do so. Once he'd settled his affairs, and when the time was right, he would pursue Him. Jesus basically replied that the time is now. Who knows what tomorrow holds. We should always put Jesus first in our lives.

The Bible teaches us that today is the day of salvation. What if there isn't a tomorrow? Did I have other worldly things to do before I made my full commitment to the Lord? Was I uninstructed on how to follow Christ? Did I let my ignorance and stubbornness permit me from doing so? Did I put Him first or last in my life? Only Jesus knew what was truly in my heart.

It's hard for a man to admit when he is wrong. As I reflect back now I wonder, did I have a false hope? Let's examine some facts. Besides knowing right from wrong, I didn't have the Holy Spirit condemning me when I sinned. The Holy Spirit now convicts me as soon as sin happens, and I confess my sins to the Lord and ask for His forgiveness. I also didn't see the importance of going to church. Keep in mind one doesn't have to go to church to be saved, but going to church refuels your spiritual batteries. Going to church prepares you to talk to the unsaved about Jesus and to learn how to walk with God, among many other things. In Hebrews 10:25, the Bible teaches us not to forsake the assembly or ourselves together.

I didn't have much of a personal relationship with Jesus, as I didn't know how to. I rarely prayed, and when I did it was mainly asking for something that I wanted. Worldly things like a new car, home, a new job; you get the picture. Prayer is communicating and listening to God. It's talking to the Lord about everything in our lives. I had experienced very few one on ones with God up to that point.

I now pray and talk with God all day long. In having a personal relationship with God, I feel "plugged in" to Him. I can also feel when I am not.

This is usually when sin is blocking the communication. I know that because I have a personal relationship with my Lord, I can ask for forgiveness and He will accept it. We have a loving God indeed.

I thought that I had fire insurance. I believed that God the Father and God the Son existed, but I left it at that. Did I believe in God or did I just believe there is a God? Let me explain. I didn't even consider the fact that even the devil himself believes in God. James 2:19 says, *Thou believest that there is one God; thou doest well: the devils also believe, and tremble.* The Bible teaches us that God made Hell for the devil and his demons. Those who reject Jesus Christ as Lord and Savior are also headed for their fiery eternal home. I thought that my small belief was enough to get me in the door of Heaven, maybe just by the skin of my teeth. I honestly believed that God would not let me, a good guy, go anywhere else but Heaven. The Bible teaches us that you cannot get to Heaven based on good deeds. I was uneducated about my eternity and blinded by the devil's lies.

I didn't know how to pray or talk to God. I tried to read the Bible but it didn't make a whole lot of sense to me. I thought that reading about creation in the Book of Genesis was interesting. I usually made it to chapter five or six, till I ran into the "begets." This is the genealogy in Genesis that takes us to Noah and the Ark. There were so many Jewish names, all hard to comprehend, that I just couldn't digest them all. It slowed me down so much that I skipped right to the end of the Bible to the Book of Revelation. At this point, I was really lost and felt so hopeless that I gave up. I tip-toed right past the New Testament and the beloved writings of Matthew, Mark, Luke, and John. I skipped right past my Lord and Savior, Jesus Christ.

As the years passed, I became more experienced with life and less of a comprehension about God. I see now that I was more interested in the physical world than the spiritual one. I had a steady girlfriend and we went to church some Sundays, but I went for all the wrong reasons. I was a teenage boy and my priorities were all out of whack. I was chasing skirts instead of following God. The truth is, I only attended because I wanted to spend time with my girlfriend.

This was undoubtedly the least favorable church to go to for a new believer. Here's what I learned at *that* church. The preacher was caught cheating with the choir director and had to resign. We didn't have a full-time preacher for the majority of the time that I attended. Shortly after that, my Sunday school teacher shot himself and committed suicide. The attendance numbers kept getting lower and lower, to the point that you hated to be next. Boy, there obviously wasn't any another reason to go there other than a girl. I can't ever remember this church preaching the Word of God. With a haughty mind I remember thinking, I need not worry about any of their problems; I had *fire insurance.*

3

Understanding What Sin Is

Sin is defined as a rebellion or disobedience against God. God originally made the world perfect in every way. The world turned corrupt the day sin entered in. Sin was first introduced when Satan first deceived Adam and Eve in the Garden of Eden. In Genesis chapter two, God gave Adam and Eve one rule. In Genesis it reads: *And the LORD God commanded the man, saying, Of every tree of the garden thou mayest freely eat: But of the tree of the knowledge of good and evil, thou shalt not eat of it: for in the day that thou eatest thereof thou shalt surely die.*

Satan convinced Eve that the tree was pleasing to the eyes. He instructed her that if she ate of the fruit, her eyes would open, and it would make her wise. The Scripture says that the serpent beguiled her and she did eat. This act was the first sin on earth. Adam ate of the fruit too, so both were guilty of sin. This act was a clear disobedience to the Lord. After Adam and Eve sinned, there was a barrier created between man and God. On that day man fell from innocence into a world of sin. Thankfully, God the Son removed the sin barrier with his shed blood at Calvary. (More on that in a moment.)

Romans 3:23 states, *All have sinned and come short of the Glory of God.* How do we know that we've sinned? In God's instruction book the Bible, He has given us the Ten Commandments. The Ten Commandments are ten laws given by God for man to follow. We find them listed in Exodus 20:

Thou shalt have no other gods before me.

Thou shalt not make unto thee any graven image, or any likeness of any thing that is in heaven above, or that is in the earth beneath, or that is in the water under the earth.

Thou shalt not bow down thyself to them, nor serve them: for I the LORD thy God am a jealous God, visiting the iniquity of the fathers upon the children unto the third and fourth generation of them that hate me;

And shewing mercy unto thousands of them that love me, and keep my commandments.

Thou shalt not take the name of the LORD thy God in vain; for the LORD will not hold him guiltless that taketh his name in vain.

Remember the sabbath day, to keep it holy. Six days shalt thou labour, and do all thy work: But the seventh day is the sabbath of the LORD thy God: in it thou shalt not do any work, thou, nor thy son, nor thy daughter, thy manservant, nor thy maidservant, nor thy cattle, nor thy stranger that is within thy gates: For in six days the LORD *made heaven and earth, the sea, and all that in them is, and rested the seventh day: wherefore the* LORD *blessed the sabbath day, and hallowed it.*

Honour thy father and thy mother: that thy days may be long upon the land which the LORD *thy God giveth thee.*

Thou shalt not kill.

Thou shalt not commit adultery.

Thou shalt not steal.

Thou shalt not bear false witness against thy neighbour.

Thou shalt not covet thy neighbour's house, thou shalt not covet thy neighbour's wife, nor his manservant, nor his maidservant, nor his ox, nor his ass, nor any thing that is thy neighbour's.

Have you ever committed even the smallest sin? The Bible states if you have broken one commandment then you have broken them all. James 2:10-11: *For whosoever shall keep the whole law, and yet offend in one point, he is guilty of all. For he that said, Do not commit adultery, said also, Do not kill. Now if thou commit no adultery, yet if thou kill, thou art become a transgressor of the law.*

We've all told those "little white lies." When I was a child, my cousins and I broke a vase at my grandmother's house. Ok, I broke a vase. When confronted about the incident I blamed my cousins. They in turn blamed me. My little fib allowed me to get out of my punishment, but at what cost?

Most have taken something that wasn't theirs. Whether it's just a pen from the office or an automobile; stealing is stealing. I remember one time when I was six years old, I shoplifted a red balloon from the grocery store. My mom caught me and made me return it. My mother was very disappointed in me and she let me know it. Lesson learned.

Jesus told us that if you lust for another in your heart you have committed adultery already. In today's times, with all the unnecessary foulness that's in television commercials, it's easy for anyone to do this and not even be aware of it. Television Executives will do anything to sell their product, even if it means putting sex, alcohol, and drugs in front of our children. It seems like there aren't any filters on television anymore, but I digress.

Have you ever dishonored your mother or father? We have all done this at some point in our life. I can think of many times in my rebellious teen years that I broke this commandment in particular.

John 3:15 says: *Whosoever hateth his brother is a murderer.* God considers hatred, murder. I know that in my past, there have been people that I have said I've hated. They have made me so upset that I had that burning hatred in my heart. I'm so thankful that God has now taken that hatred out of my life.

Have you ever wanted something so bad that you've put this reward above God? God should always be first in your life. Lifting an item above God is a sin. Whether it be a job, a relationship, money, a nice home, or a fancy car, always put God first in your life. The list goes on and on. As you can see, here are just a few examples of breaking God's Commandments, or God's law. No matter how great or small your shortcomings are, God considers sin just that; sin.

Don't forget the sins of omission. James 4:17 says: *Therefore to him that knoweth to do good, and doeth it not, to him it is sin.* A sin of omission would be *not* doing something God's Word teaches us that we should do. An example of a sin of omission would be: If you see someone in need and you do not help them because it might not be convenient for you at the time. It could be as simple as not sharing the Gospel with a nonbeliever. Maybe one is called to serve the Lord at his church, but feels that the Sunday football game is more important than Sunday's Church service. Whatever the sin may be, Romans 3:10 sums it up: *As it is written, There is none righteous, no, not one.*

Now that we have determined we are all sinners, what can we do? 1st John 1:9 makes it clear: *If we confess our sins, he is faithful and just to forgive us our sins, and to cleanse us from all unrighteousness.* God will cleanse us of all sins, no matter how immoral. All we have to do is ask Him to forgive us. Micah 7:19 says: *He will turn again, he will have compassion upon us; he will subdue our iniquities; and thou wilt cast all their sins into the depths of the sea.* We serve a loving God that is faithful and just to forgive us. All we have to do is submit to Him and ask for forgiveness. He will take all your sins and toss them into the deepest parts of the sea where they will be forgotten forever.

Before the coming of Christ, God required animal sacrifices to provide a temporary covering of sins. (Leviticus 4:35, 5:10). When Jesus came into this world, He became the ultimate sacrifice for all our transgressions. 2nd Corinthians 5:21 says: *For he hath made him to be sin for us, who knew no sin; that we might be made the righteousness of God in him.* Jesus Christ died on the cross for you and for me. He bore our sins of the world so we would not go to a devil's Hell. All we have to do is ask for forgiveness of our sins, know that Jesus paid the price for our sins on the cross, and follow Him.

What happens after we accept Jesus as our Savior? John 14:16-17 shows us: *And I will pray the Father, and he shall give you another Comforter, that he may abide with you for ever; Even the Spirit of truth; whom the world cannot receive, because it seeth him not, neither knoweth him: but ye know him; for he dwelleth with you, and shall be in you.* The Holy Spirit takes up residency in your heart. Jesus calls the Holy Spirit the "Comforter," the "Holy Ghost," and the "Spirit of Truth." The Holy Spirit is the third part of the Holy Trinity. Ephesians 4:30 tells us: *And grieve not the Holy Spirit of God, whereby ye are sealed unto the day of redemption.* The Holy Spirit convicts us of our sins, enabling us to ask the Father for forgiveness. John 16:13 *Howbeit when he, the Spirit of truth, is come, he will guide you into all truth: for he shall not speak of himself; but whatsoever he shall hear, that shall he speak: and he will shew you things to come.* We must receive what Jesus promised us; an indwelling of the Holy Spirit. The Holy Spirit will lead us, help us, and guide us along our Christian journey.

It is human nature to sin. We will not be perfect even after we are saved. The difference is that we are now covered by the saving blood of Jesus Christ. Jesus told the believer that He will never leave or forsake us. When you get down and out and feel like you don't have a friend left in the world, remember these words of encouragement: Jesus will always be with you. Turn to Jesus now and forevermore. He will give you the guidance you seek. Remember that just because we are saved doesn't make us sinless, but we should strive to sin less.

4

God Has a Plan

God has given everyone a purpose in life. Genesis 1:27 says: *So God created man in his own image, in the image of God created he him; male and female created he them.* If God allowed you to be born, He has a purpose for you. We are all souls, created in God's image with infinite potential. Have you ever wondered, "What is God's purpose for me?" What does He want me to accomplish in the short time that I have here on earth? It took years before I was prepared to tackle this question.

I decided to look to the Word of God for my answer. In Ephesians 5:1-2 it says: *Be ye therefore followers of God, as dear children; and walk in love, as Christ also hath loved us.* In Deuteronomy 13:4 His Word tells us this: *Ye shall walk after the L*ORD *your God, and fear him, and keep his commandments, and obey his voice, and ye shall serve him, and cleave unto him.* God tells us our purpose in life is to walk with Him and to serve Him here on earth and in Heaven. He tells us in Psalms 32:8: *I will instruct thee and teach thee in* *the way which thou shalt go: I will guide thee with mine eye.*

We sometimes fall short of our goals in life, but God still sees the great potential in all of us. John 15:2-4 explains to us that if we work with God, He will guide us and show us the right path. *Every branch in me that beareth not fruit he taketh away: and every branch that beareth fruit, he purgeth it, that it may bring forth more fruit. Now ye are clean through the word which I have spoken unto you. Abide in me, and I in you. As the branch cannot bear fruit of itself, except it abide in the vine; no more can ye, except ye abide in me.*

God is our great gardener. He is the vine and you are the branch. He trims the things in your life that prohibit you from reaching your full potential. As you start to grow or "bud" in your personal relationship with Him, trials may take place. God permits these trials to happen so that you will draw closer to Him.

God will also "prune the weeds out of the garden", allowing you to thrive to your fullest potential. He wants you to have a deep, close, and intimate relationship with Him. It all starts by talking with God. We have a phenomenal and all powerful God that still takes the time to hear our prayers. He is the Creator of the universe, all knowing and all powerful, and yet He takes the time to hear me when I call out to Him. We have a truly loving God indeed.

As you pray, God will reveal to you how He wants you to better serve Him. God blesses everyone with gifts to be able to serve and reach your full potential. These gifts are blessings from God. It is up to you to utilize these talents from the Lord. He might call you to the mission fields to preach the Gospel, or He might simply have you teach a Sunday school class at your local church. Some people are blessed with a beautiful singing voice, while others have the gift of gab. Whatever your gift is, God will reveal this to you. He wants you to serve Him, and serve Him faithfully. By doing His will, you give God the glory He deserves.

You may think, "I have no special talents or gifts from God, how can I serve Him?" Everyone can pray, right? We can offer glory to God by praying. Psalms 103 1:5 says: *Bless the LORD, O my soul: and all that is within me, bless his holy name. Bless the LORD, O my soul, and forget not all his benefits: Who forgiveth all thine iniquities; who healeth all thy diseases; Who redeemeth thy life from destruction; who crowneth thee with lovingkindness and tender mercies; Who satisfieth thy mouth with good things; so that thy youth is renewed like the eagle's.* As you do God's will, you will draw closer to Him.

The Lord does not want us to waste our talents. For example, let's say a young girl at church has a remarkable singing voice, but never uses it to exalt the Lord, then she is being slothful.

God wants us to use our talents/gifts to glorify Him. Romans 12:11 says: *Not slothful in business; fervent in spirit; serving the Lord.* Simply put: Serve the Lord passionately and with all your heart. He is our Lord, give Him the glory He righteously deserves.

Praying is one of the greatest things a Christian can do to glorify the Lord. Prayer is a great tool to use in your walk of life. It is a way to talk to God on a personal level. Through prayer, God will show you the way. Psalms 32:8 says: *I will instruct thee and teach thee in the way which thou shalt go: I will guide thee with mine eye.* John 4:23 tells us we need to worship the Father in spirit and in truth.

The good news is our God is a loving God. Even though I was stiff necked and didn't know how to grow as a Christian, He still loved me and had a plan for me. I tried to mature spiritually when I was younger but failed miserably. I tried reading the Bible, but to no avail. Due to my lack of faith, I didn't understand it and quickly gave up. I tried praying too. The problem with that is I didn't know how to pray effectively. I had only heard grace a few times in my life. The only other prayer I heard was from the preacher at the basketball game. I didn't go to church till much later. When I did go, I picked the wrong church. This church didn't preach the Word of God. It was more of a Sunday get together in the name of God.

In Revelation 3:20, Jesus sends us a powerful message: *Behold, I stand at the door, and knock: if any man hear my voice, and open the door, I will come in to him, and will sup with him, and he with me.* The word "behold" means to give your attention. Jesus says to behold or listen up. He has taken the initiative to get your attention, because He has something very important to tell you that will change your life for eternity. He is willing to change your heart if you are willing to open the door. If you notice He doesn't tear the door down in this Scripture, He simply taps. He's at the door ready to enter into your heart if you are willing to accept Him.

The next part of the Scripture says, *"If any man hear my voice and open the door, I will come in to him, and sup with him, and he with me."* If you let Jesus into your life, He will fellowship with you. He will not only be your Savior, but also your friend. Whatever circumstances arise in your life, Jesus will be right there with you. He understands every fear, pain, sorrow, and tear shed, along with every good thing that you experience in your life. Listen to Him and He will guide you in life's journey.

Many unsaved hear Jesus knocking at the door, yet fail to open it. Some let pride, stubbornness, and arrogance stand in the way of accepting God. Jesus will never force you to open the door. When He calls, it's up to you to listen. God has given all of us the freewill to make our own decisions. If the unsaved knew and understood what the future holds without Jesus Christ, they would want to be saved today.

Once Jesus enters your life, He changes everything from your eternal destination to your daily walk with Him. It is imperative to open the door and let Him in. Only then will you experience life to the fullest; trusting in the knowledge that Jesus Christ is Lord.

I could hear Jesus knocking on my heart's door, but I was too involved in my daily activities to put God first. Please be aware, it is possible to lead a life that is blinded to the truth. This is one of the devils greatest deceits. The devil can blind your eyes from the light which is Jesus Christ. He wants to push you away from God anyway he can. Don't be so consumed with worldly pleasures that you let this deceit pull you under.

Some may think, "I don't have time in my busy schedule for God." Some would rather watch a ball game then go to the Lord's house on Sunday. Let me ask you this: If you have a girlfriend or wife, would you only spend one hour a week or less with them? How much greater then is the Lord?

God even had a plan for me. He brought me out of a situation where His Word wasn't preached respectfully. Well, it wasn't preached much at all. If you liked to play bingo, this was your church.

God also allowed me to meet my beautiful wife. He brought me through a very difficult and personal time that changed my life forever; which paved the way for my spiritual walk with Him. He gave me guidance and direction when I needed Him the most. God doesn't allow anything to happen by accident or happenstance. He has a plan for everyone. His plan for me was starting to unfold right before my very eyes.

5

What is Heaven Like?

While in Sunday church service, I recently had a thought about my grandma and grandpa. Someone was singing a song about Heaven with the lyrics: "How I wish you were here." I started thinking deeply about my grandparents, who are both in Heaven. As I drifted away in the song, I could see them both so clear. They were walking by an old beaten path, along a lakeside. I envisioned every detail. They were both so young, maybe in their twenties. I could distinctly see my grandma's face; there were no wrinkles. In my observation, I thought that perhaps I stepped back in time. She had short black hair, and her glittering eyes danced off the water. She wore a white cotton dress and had a daisy fixed in her hair. Grandpa had a full head of red and brown hair, and his stature was like that of a movie star. They were both smiling while walking hand in hand. It seemed so peaceful. The lake looked like watercolors being brushed on in a painting. It was so bright, and everything looked fresh and new. They were very happy together, with love in their eyes as they walked along the shore line. It was so wonderful to think of them in that way. This thought made me look closer into the question, "What is Heaven really like, according to God's Word?"

We've all seen movies that portray Heaven as a place high up in the clouds, where angels play harps, while donning sparkling white linen robes. A place where believers go to spend eternity: with peace, joy, and happiness all around them. While some of that might be true; the truth is, we know very little about what Heaven is like based on what's written in the Bible.

In the Book of Revelation, John reveals to us some clues about the hereafter. Heaven is described in the Bible as a beautiful place, a perfect place; Paradise. In Revelation 21:2 John sees a city in Heaven called the New Jerusalem. Revelation 21:21 describes the city as having pearly white gates and having streets of gold as it were transparent glass. Revelation 21:22 states that God Almighty and Jesus Christ are the temple in the city. In Revelation 16:17, John is describing Heaven as a place where the people shall never go hungry, thirst, or cry tears or sorrow. *They shall hunger no more, neither thirst any more; neither shall the sun light on them, nor any heat. For the Lamb which is in the midst of the throne shall feed them, and shall lead them unto living fountains of waters: and God shall wipe away all tears from their eyes.* John goes on to tell us that in this great city there is no need for the sun or moon, because the Glory of God is the light. God will not allow anything to enter Heaven that is not righteous. The wicked will not be permitted. Revelation 21:27 says: *And there shall in no wise enter into it any thing that defileth, neither whatsoever worketh abomination, or maketh a lie: but they which are written in the Lamb's book of life.*

What will we do in Heaven? There is some Scripture that relates to what we will be doing in Heaven once we arrive. The Bible says that we will be praising and worshiping the Father. It also mentions that there will be music, rejoicing, singing, and eating in Heaven. We will see our loved ones and fellowship in Heaven. It also says that we will see the face of the Father. Spending an eternity in a Paradise that was designed by our Creator, sounds like "Heaven" to me.

Where is Jesus, and what will He be doing in Heaven? Jesus did not leave us to simply go to Heaven and take a break. He left to do the will of the Father. Jesus tells us in John 14:2-3: *In my Father's house are many mansions: if it were not so, I would have told you. I go to prepare a place for you. And if I go and prepare a place for you, I will come again, and receive you unto myself; that where I am, there ye may be also.* While it's not clear if Jesus is talking about our new heavenly bodies as homes, or our very own personal mansion; it is clear that when His work is done, He will come again and take us with Him.

According to Scripture, Jesus will be standing on the right hand of the Father and interceding for our transgressions. Romans 8:34 tells us: *Who is he that condemneth? It is Christ that died, yea rather, that is risen again, who is even at the right hand of God, who also maketh intercession for us.* 1John 2:1 speaks on this: *My little children, these things write I unto you, that ye sin not. And if any man sin, we have an advocate with the Father, Jesus Christ the righteous:* Jesus is actively pleading our case to the Father. Jesus went to the cross of Calvary to pay our sin debt. Our Father does not look at our sins or transgressions, but at the righteousness of our Savior.

All of God's children will one day have a new body in Heaven with no pain, disease, or sickness. In Revelation 21:4, John tells us: *And God shall wipe away all tears from their eyes; and there shall be no more death, neither sorrow, nor crying, neither shall there be any more pain: for the former things are passed away.*

In Deuteronomy 29:29, God reveals to us that the secret things belong to Him. God lets us know in this verse that He doesn't reveal everything to us. Some things are left mysterious for a reason. We must have faith in God's work and eternal plan. Don't be discouraged with not knowing everything about Heaven. If my daydream isn't exactly what Heaven will be like, I know it will be wonderful place. We worship a merciful God, and He allows us to enter a great reward that we do not deserve. Put your faith in

Him for your eternal salvation. He has grand and glorious things in store for the believer here on earth and in Heaven.

6

We Have a Loving God

It was the day of my girlfriend's high school graduation. We had been together for over three years, and we felt pretty comfortable in our relationship to say the least. I was dealing with a major conflict in my plans for the day. Many months before her graduation day was announced, I had a fishing trip planned for that day. I was working two jobs, so time was very valuable to me. Being a young stubborn guy, my mind was made up to go fishing.

Her graduating class was so big that it would take at least five hours to make it through the ceremony. Five hours I could be fishing. I just graduated from the same school the year before, and graduation lasted all day long. I didn't want to sit through it again if I didn't have to. She was pretty upset about it and looking back now, I guess I can understand why.

At the last minute, something changed my mind. I cancelled my fishing plans and decided to surprise her by showing up. I didn't see what the big deal was, but I wanted to support her. I arrived early to the venue where the graduation was being held. I saw my girlfriend standing at the front door, talking to her friends before the ceremony started.

As I approached her, she seemed startled. She stumbled on her words but managed to get out, "Wha- what are you doing here? You can't be here." She now had a panicked look on her face. I told her, "I decided to show up, besides you only graduate high school once, right?" She looked at her friends, then back at me. She then did something that totally shocked me. She asked me to leave. She said I wasn't allowed in. Confused, I said, "Why don't you want me here?" She said with a painful chatter, "I brought someone else to the graduation. I brought…..another guy."

My fists clinched with fury. I gathered myself and smoothly said, "Ok point him out to me." I glared all around, trying to find him in the large crowd. I figured he would be sitting beside her family. In my younger days I was a bit hot-tempered, touchy, and short-fused. I later found out she'd been seeing this other guy for months. She turned towards me and said with one last plea, "Stop it. You will not ruin my graduation day. Leave right now." I thought for a quick second and then said, "You're right. And by the way….we're done!" I stormed past her and her friends and headed back to my car.

On my way to the car I passed a familiar face. I heard a loud voice shout from the distance, "Hey!" This was a good friend from high school. I remembered walking past her about three steps before I suddenly stopped. The thought ran across my mind, "I'm single now...."

A few years later, the same girl who took the time to say "hey" to me, discussed her graduation day. It turns out we saw things very differently. It was almost noon with the sun glaring down on us, so I was wearing sunglasses. She thought I was looking right at her as I was heading to my car. Truth is, I didn't see her at all. I turned around and had a few minute conversation with her. She joked around about a guy who fell off the stage during graduation rehearsal the day before. I teased her that I would be looking in tomorrow's newspaper for a girl falling off the stage. We discussed going to college in the fall. I told her that I signed up for some classes and I hoped to see her there sometime. That was about it I guess. I was trying to hide the fact that I was still fuming from that days previous events.

I needed to clear my mind so I decided to take that fishing trip. While fishing, all I could think about was my good friend that I had spoken to at graduation. The past girlfriend and her mysterious beau were clear out of my mind at this point.

It took me two weeks to find her phone number. I've never called a girl out of the blue. I was always the guy that the girls called first. I didn't know what to say. I started contemplating ideas. I remembered her telling a story at the lunch table, about how she used to babysit for my little cousin. I also had knowledge that she went to the same church my uncle did. Bingo! I would ask for an invitation to church on Sunday. I knew that was my ticket for conversation, so I made the phone call.

We started our conversation out with pleasantries and hopes for the upcoming fall semester. We spoke for a few more minutes. This was enough time for me to work up the courage to ask her to go to church with me on Sunday. "I've been thinking about going to church. Are you still a member of the church that my uncle goes too? Would it be alright if I went with you on Sunday?"

I did want to go to church, that was true. I also wanted to go with her. I knew the previous church that I attended was the wrong church to go to, but it was church. I figured that if I went to church with someone that came from a good family and had good moral values, perhaps I would find the answers I was seeking. Was I wanting to go just for that reason? Well let's just say it was 50/50.

To my surprise, she turned me down. I hadn't planned for that. After all, I was the guy that the girls always called. It never crossed my mind that she might say no. I didn't know how to continue our conversation. I didn't know to be mad or upset, because she didn't give me a reason. She just said no. I thought, "Who would refuse to go to church with a friend?" There had to be more to the story. Then it crossed my mind. I figured she probably had a boyfriend and that might be a little awkward. With nothing to lose I asked about her dating status. She mumbled, "I'm single." I was stumped.

After several failed attempts on my part to find out why she didn't want to go with me on Sunday, she confessed. She informed me that she just had her wisdom teeth pulled and was very swollen and bruised. It took a little convincing, but I won her over.

This was a new beginning for me in several different ways. I finally had the chance to hear God's Word. There was opportunity here to have two budding relationships; a new girlfriend and a new relationship with God Almighty through His preached Gospel each Sunday. God lead me to His Word in a very different way, and it was now up to me understand it.

7

Jesus Christ, My Savior

Now seek the LORD your God with all your heart and soul. **1 Chronicles 22:19 (NLT)**

I would like to tell you a story about a man who is very important to me. This man is unlike any other; He is perfect in every way. He is a spectacular teacher and mentor to all that seek Him. He performed many astounding miracles during His public ministry on earth such as healing the blind, raising the dead, casting out demons, and walking on water. He also healed the sick and paralyzed, turned water into wine, and fed five thousand with only five barley loaves and two fishes. He did so many great and wonderful things during His ministry, which was over two thousand years ago, that people still talk about Him today. He knows the past, present, future, and has unlimited power over all creation. This man is very special to every Christian that has ever lived. He did something for me that I'll never be able to repay. He died for my sins, so that I can live again. His name is Jesus Christ. He is my Savior and my best friend.

Christianity is centered round the belief that Jesus Christ died on the cross for the sins of everyone, and rose again after three days. Anyone that wants to be a Christian must repent of their sins, put their faith and trust in Christ, and have a relationship with Him. Having a close personal relationship with Jesus is His ultimate purpose for creating you. God devised this plan of salvation for everyone, because He loves us and wants us to spend eternity with Him.

You cannot buy your way into Heaven. Good works will not get you there either. There is only one way to Heaven, and that's having faith in the shed blood of Jesus Christ. God sent his Son Jesus to earth some two thousand years ago to be the sacrificial lamb for all our transgressions.

Jesus Christ's sacrifice on the cross was sufficient in the eyes of God. There is nothing man can do alone to make it to Heaven. We must accept God's plan of salvation, and believe on Jesus as Savior. The Bible clearly tells us in John 14:6 that Jesus Christ is the only way: *Jesus saith unto him, I am the way, the truth, and the life: no man cometh unto the Father, but by me.*

There are many people today who lack knowledge about our Savior Jesus Christ. I used to be one of them. I was a newly converted Christian, yet I didn't know how to have a personal relationship with Him. I really didn't know who Christ was, other than someone told me He was the

Son of God. I lacked instruction on how to grow as a Christian. I didn't know how to have that personal walk with Him. Let's face it, I was missing out. It would be like having a relationship with your best friend and never talking. If someone had this type of relationship, they definitely would be missing on so many great things.

So what do you know about Jesus Christ? A lot of people might only know that He is the Son of God and not much else. I was once that guy so I can relate. I eventually opened my Bible and started reading it. After reading the Gospels, I realized how great my Savior really is. I would like to share some Scripture and knowledge with you that might give you better understanding of who Jesus Christ is, where He came from, and how to have a close personal relationship with Him.

Many people think that Jesus did not come onto the scene until the New Testament. Physically this might be true, but Jesus Christ is part of the Holy Trinity. He has been with us since the beginning of existence. This is explained in John 1:1-14 (NLT), which reads: *In the beginning the word already existed. The Word was with God, and the Word was God. He existed in the beginning with God. God created everything through him, and nothing was created except through him. The Word gave life to everything that was created, and his life brought light to everyone. The light shines in the darkness, and the darkness can never extinguish it. God sent a man, John the*

Baptist, to tell about the light so that everyone might believe because of his testimony. John himself was not the light; he was simply a witness to tell about the light. The one who is the true light, who gives light to everyone, was coming into the world. He came into the very world he created, but the world didn't recognize him. He came to his own people, and even they rejected him. But to all who believed him and accepted him, he gave the right to become children of God. They are reborn—not with a physical birth resulting from human passion or plan, but a birth that comes from God. So the Word became human and made his home among us. He was full of unfailing love and faithfulness. And we have seen his glory, the glory of the Father's one and only Son.

Once you read through the Bible, you will see that Jesus is not only in the New Testament, but He is also very real in the Old Testament. There are many references to Jesus Christ in the Old Testament, starting with the Book of Genesis. Here are just a few examples: Genesis 1:26: *And God said, Let us make man in our image, after our likeness: and let them have dominion over the fish of the sea, and over the fowl of the air, and over the cattle, and over all the earth, and over every creeping thing that creepeth upon the earth.* God is speaking of the Holy Trinity in this verse: God the Father, God the Son, and God the Holy Spirit.

In Genesis 3:15: *And I will put enmity between thee and the woman, and between thy seed and her seed; it shall bruise thy head, and thou shalt bruise his heel.* This is the first prophecy of the coming of Christ and his glorious works. Notice that this passage does not say that the "seed" came from Adam. It speaks about the virgin birth. It is more clearly revealed in Isaiah 7:14: *Therefore the Lord himself shall give you a sign; Behold, a virgin shall conceive, and bear a son, and shall call his name Immanuel.* The New Testament also calls Jesus the seed in Galatians 3:16.

"He shall bruise your head, and you shall bruise His heel. This passage refers to the defeat of Satan by the coming of Jesus. God is drawing the battle lines between Himself and Satan. Satan is defeated by the cross of Christ. Jesus is the victor.

I have no doubt that Jesus Christ is the Messiah. There are over three hundred Old Testament prophecies of the coming Messiah, and all were fulfilled by Jesus Christ. Each time I read an Old Testament prophecy I am truly amazed at the truth of His Word. Here are just a few Old Testament prophecies that prove to everyone; Jesus Christ is the Messiah:

1. Isaiah 9:7 shares that the Messiah will be heir to the throne of David. This prophecy is fulfilled in Matthew 1:1 with a record of the genealogy of Jesus Christ; the son of David.

2. Isaiah 7:14 states the coming Messiah will be virgin born. This prophecy was fulfilled in the Book of Luke.

3. Micah 5:2 says the coming Messiah will be born in Bethlehem. This is fulfilled in Matthew 2:1

4. Zechariah 9:9 states: *Rejoice greatly, O daughter of Zion; shout, O daughter of Jerusalem: behold, thy King cometh unto thee: he is just, and having salvation; lowly, and riding upon an ass, and upon a colt the foal of an ass.* This prophecy was fulfilled in Matthew 21:7-9.

5. Isaiah 53:3 states that He would be despised and rejected by His own people. This was fulfilled in John 1:11: *He came unto his own, and his own received him not.*

6. Jesus would be betrayed by a friend. Psalms 41:9: *Yea, mine own familiar friend, in whom I trusted, which did eat of my bread, hath lifted up his heel against me.* This prophecy came true in the Book of Mark 14:17-18, 22.

7. Christ would be betrayed for thirty pieces of silver. This is shown in Zechariah 11:12: *And I said unto them, If ye think good, give me my price; and if not, forbear. So they weighed for my price thirty pieces of silver.* This prophecy came to fruition in the Book of Matthew 26.

8. Zechariah 11:13 states that the thirty pieces of silver would be returned to the potter's field. This also came true in Matthew 27.

9. Psalms 27:12 tells us that Jesus would be accused by false witnesses. It reads: *Deliver me not over unto the will of mine enemies: for false witnesses are risen up against me, and such as*

breathe out cruelty. This New Testament fulfillment is showed to us in Matthew 26:59-60.

10. Isaiah 53:7 tells us the Messiah would be silent in front of his accusers. It reads: *He was oppressed, and he was afflicted, yet he opened not his mouth: he is brought as a lamb to the slaughter, and as a sheep before her shearers is dumb, so he openeth not his mouth.* This too is fulfilled in Matthew 27:12-14 which reads: *And when he was accused of the chief priests and elders, he answered nothing. Then said Pilate unto him, Hearest thou not how many things they witness against thee? And he answered him to never a word; insomuch that the governor marvelled greatly.*

11. He would die for our sins. Isaiah 53:5-8 reads: *But he was wounded for our transgressions, he was bruised for our iniquities: the chastisement of our peace was upon him; and with his stripes we are healed. All we like sheep have gone astray; we have turned every one to his own way; and the LORD hath laid on him the iniquity of us all. He was oppressed, and he was afflicted, yet he opened not his mouth: he is brought as a lamb to the slaughter, and as a sheep before her shearers is dumb, so he openeth not his mouth. He was taken from prison and from judgment: and who shall declare his generation? for he was cut off out of the land of the living: for the transgression of my people was he stricken.* Prophecy was fulfilled when Christ died on the cross for our sins. In

Romans 5:8 the writer tells us that while we were still sinners, Christ died for us.

12. None of the Messiah's bones would be broken. Psalms 34:20 reads: *He keepeth all his bones: not one of them is broken.* This prophecy was fulfilled in John 19: 33-36, which reads: *But when they came to Jesus, and saw that he was dead already, they brake not his legs: But one of the soldiers with a spear pierced his side, and forthwith came there out blood and water. And he that saw it bare record, and his record is true: and he knoweth that he saith true, that ye might believe. For these things were done, that the scripture should be fulfilled, A bone of him shall not be broken.*

King David wrote a Psalm that is very dear to my heart. After reading Psalms 22 for the first time, I thought, "How could anyone not believe in Jesus as Lord?" In Psalms 22, David writes about the crucifixion of Jesus. Psalms 22 was written over one thousand years before it happened, yet this sounds like a cry of anguish from David. With this graphic description of the crucifixion of Jesus, one would think David was personally present at the cross that day. Psalms 22 reads:

My God, my God, why hast thou forsaken me? why art thou so far from helping me, and from the words of my roaring? O my God, I cry in the day time, but thou hearest not; and in the night season, and am not silent. But thou art holy, O thou that inhabitest the praises of Israel. Our fathers trusted in thee: they trusted, and thou didst deliver them. They cried unto thee, and were delivered: they trusted in thee, and were not confounded. But I am a worm, and no man; a reproach of men, and despised of the people. All they that see me laugh me to scorn: they shoot out the lip, they shake the head, saying, He trusted on the LORD that he would deliver him: let him deliver him, seeing he delighted in him. But thou art he that took me out of the womb: thou didst make me hope when I was upon my mother's breasts. I was cast upon thee from the womb: thou art my God from my mother's belly. Be not far from me; for trouble is near; for there is none to help. Many bulls have compassed me: strong bulls of Bashan have beset me round. They gaped upon me with their mouths, as a ravening and a roaring lion. I am poured out like water, and all my bones are out of joint: my heart is like wax; it is melted in the midst of my bowels. My strength is dried up like a potsherd; and my tongue cleaveth to my jaws; and thou hast brought me into the dust of death. For dogs have compassed me: the assembly of the wicked have inclosed me: they pierced my hands and my feet. I may tell all my bones: they look and stare upon me. They part my garments among them, and cast lots upon my vesture. But be not thou far from me, O LORD: O my strength, haste thee to help me. Deliver my soul from the sword; my darling from the power of the dog. Save me from the lion's mouth: for thou hast heard me from the horns of the unicorns. I will declare thy name unto my brethren: in the midst of the congregation will I praise thee. Ye that fear the LORD, *praise him; all ye the seed of Jacob, glorify him; and fear him, all ye the seed of Israel. For he hath not despised nor abhorred the affliction of the afflicted; neither hath he hid his face from him; but when he cried unto him, he heard. My praise shall be of thee in the great congregation: I will pay my vows before them that fear him. The meek shall eat and be satisfied: they shall praise the* LORD *that seek him: your heart shall live for ever. All the ends of the world shall remember and turn unto the* LORD: *and all the kindreds of the nations shall worship before thee. For the kingdom is the* LORD's: *and he is the governor among the nations. All they that be fat upon earth shall eat and worship: all they that go down to the dust shall bow before him: and none can keep alive his own soul. A seed shall serve him; it shall be accounted to the Lord for a generation. They shall come, and shall declare his righteousness unto a people that shall be born, that he hath done this.*

As Christians grow in spiritual maturity, we hunger for an intimate relationship with Jesus. At the same time we might feel confused on how to achieve this. I didn't grow up in the church. I lacked instruction and knowledge of how to have a personal and intimate relationship with Jesus Christ. Through time, God has revealed to me how to have the relationship I was seeking with Him. I would like to share the knowledge that I've learned while believing in Christ as my Savior, on how to have a close meaningful relationship with Him:

1. We must trust in Him. Proverbs 3:5 says: *Trust in the LORD with all thine heart; and lean not unto thine own understanding.* Developing a relationship involves trust. Trust in Jesus with all decisions in life, no matter how small or great.

2. Read and study the Bible. John chapter one shares with us: In the beginning was the Word. The Word was with God, and the Word was God. The Word was made flesh and dwelt among us, therefore reading God's Word is communing with Him. We need to have a fellowship, harmony, togetherness, closeness, and unity.

3. Put God first in your life. With today's hectic life, we can fall into certain traps and start neglecting what matters most; which is Jesus Christ. We must be 100% honest about everything when talking to God. If you put Jesus first in your life, you will soon find that everything else will fall right into place.

4. Sharing your faith with others. Jesus instructed His disciples to go out and preach the Gospel to all nations. By sharing the Christian faith with others, you are doing God's will. When

you are doing the things God instructs you to do, your relationship with Him grows even stronger.

5. The Bible instructs us to pray without ceasing. Pray to God the Father in the name of Jesus. Tell Him about your daily accomplishments, struggles, heartaches, and your wants and needs. He already knows these things but wants you to open up to Him. Having a strong prayer relationship with God is very important in my life. When I call upon my Lord, He listens to me. He hears what I have to say. I used to think of Him as a super natural being, high up in the Heavens, ruling the worlds with infinite power. Now I call on Him as my friend. Someone I can turn to, no matter the circumstance. He is my best friend and my Savior.

Jesus develops an intimate relationship with those are willing to walk righteously before Him. Trust and obey His Word. Give Him the glory and respect that He deserves. Without my relationship with Jesus, I know I would be lost. Jesus is so much a part of my life now. He is my Savior and my best friend. When I wake up in the morning till I lay down at night; He is on my mind.

8

Time Marches On

As the next few years followed, the girl I once called "goofy cute" from high school, was now my fiancé. She wasn't goofy cute at all; quite the opposite really. She was so beautiful inside and out. I just told her that because I knew it would get under her skin a little. What a way to flirt. I also knew that God was with her, which made her more beautiful to me. Anyways, we didn't date in high school but we were good friends.

I recall doing each other's homework on our lunch break. We had a guitar class together; I would do her guitar worksheets and she would finish my English homework. I've always been musically gifted and was especially good at the guitar. I played lead guitar in several bands over the years. Let's politely say guitar wasn't her thing. One thing that attracted me to her was her book smarts. It seemed like on our lunch together, I was always quizzing her on her Latin vocabulary assignments. I also knew that her dad was in the military, so I used to go after lunch to the army and navy recruiters and get brochures. I would hand them to her as we passed in the hall or on the school bus ride home, just to have something to talk about. She thought I wanted to ship her off to the navy. I just wanted to be close to her.

During our first couple months of dating, I realized I would have to find a real job if I ever thought of marrying her. I had been doing a couple online classes at the university and I was working two part-time jobs. She was going to school full-time and also working a part time job. I started thinking about my future and I wanted her in it.

"What kind of job could I do that I would enjoy and make a lot of money at?" Since I was only a year out of high school, I didn't think that job existed. I looked to the newspaper for answers. There in the paper, I saw two ads for car salesmen. "Make forty-thousand dollars in your first year. No experience necessary." That was enough to get my attention. I loved cars. I had a Chevrolet C10 pickup and a Chevrolet Camaro that I was always tinkering with. My cousin and I had replaced motors, transmissions, and all the rest; trying to make these vehicles like new again. I went the very next day to the closest dealership that was in the ad. I set down with the manager and told him I loved cars and had rebuilt several of them in high school. I would love the opportunity to sale them. The manager hired me right on the spot. I was so excited for this new opportunity. I thought that if I could make forty thousand dollars a year selling cars, I could start planning for a future with my love. I later found out that the owner had just passed away the week before, and all the sales people besides one, had quit. They would have hired anybody. God provided this opportunity for me to sell cars. He allowed for me a way to brighten my future and secure myself financially. There wasn't any other explanation. God is good.

Taking advantage of a misfortune, I was given the extra attention needed from the managers to succeed. Taking me under their wing, they took the time to explain to me all the ins and outs of making a sale. I became very good at my job; quickly. I made more my first week selling cars then I had the whole month before; working my other two part-time jobs. I soon decided that this job was for me and so I quit college. That was a decision I now regret. It's not that I yearn to be a teacher, but I missed out on the education. My mindset was this: The faster I could make lots of money and prove myself the better. I cut some major corners in my life searching for the almighty dollar. I wanted to show everyone I could be a leader, but I soon lost focus of what my goal was. It went from wanting to provide for a better future, to being greedy and money minded. In order to prove that I made it, I thought that I needed to buy fancy cars and bigger houses. I thought that obtaining these things would mean I was someone. I put my wants above what mattered most; which is serving God. 1 John 2:15 says: *Love not the world, neither the things that are in the world. If any man love the world, the love of the Father is not in him.*

My fiancé and I soon married and moved into our first home. It was fixed in a remote neighborhood outside of town. We found a great starter home which consisted of a three bedroom, one and a half bath, one car garage. It even had a mini backyard for children to play in. This was a nice neighborhood and seemed very tranquil. In my mind, this was the first step in showing that I had made it. I wasn't born into money, so I was out to prove to everyone that I am more than just something; I wanted to be on top of the world.

My wife thought that the church we were attending was too big, and she didn't feel like she fit in there. This church usually had more than three hundred in attendance on Sunday morning. I had gone there over three years, and I really didn't know anyone except my Sunday school teachers. I still liked our church and the people that attended. I was comfortable going to this church. It felt like the right place to be.

My wife was on the nose in the sense that it felt like we'd lost that intimate touch in attending a large church. She'd missed the mark about one thing though. She made her mind up for the both of us that we were changing churches without ever discussing it openly. We did talk about it, but her mind was already made up. She thought that I would just follow her, but I didn't want change. I was just now getting comfortable in a church that I knew was a true church of God. This was not some place of worship posing as a church, like I had gone to before. I was also still spiritually immature and didn't fully understand why she wanted to change churches. Looking back now it was the right move for us. I didn't see till much later that this too was part of God's plan.

My wife had told me she wanted to find an old country church fixated on a hilltop, with about fifty people in attendance. One with a white picket fence in the front yard and a cemetery that we can be buried in once we pass on. She wanted to find a church where everyone knew each other's names and could fellowship more closely with one another. I didn't see anything wrong with our current church. After all, we said our wedding vows at this church. I felt I had made a connection there.

My wife had heard good things about a small church, only a few miles down the road from our house. I was head strong and single minded, and didn't want to go to any church that wasn't the one we were married at. While trying to come up with a reason not to attend, I realized that our dealership was open from noon till five on Sundays. I used this as an excuse not to go. I did have to work most of those Sundays, but when I didn't I used the excuse that I was too tired. I let pride and arrogance stand in the way of God's Word. I instantly became part of the "I only go to Church on Easter and Christmas" crowd.

A year after I started in sales, I moved into a team leader position. This was the first time that a team leader would be used at our dealership. I remember talking to my manager about the position. "You've taught me so well. I love my job. I'm good at everything my job requires. The only thing I need help on is closing the deal, but I know that will come in time. What exactly does a team leader do anyways?" I'll never forget, the manager had a bewildered look on his face as he said to me, "You will be closing all the car deals for your team." He must have had more faith in my closing abilities than I did. He asked me if I still wanted the position. I told him yes. I wanted to learn the art of closing a deal correctly, and I knew that this was just the ticket for me to do so.

Over the next couple of years I won numerous awards with my closing abilities. I also made a lot of money. Great things were happening very quickly in my life. I went from a poor teen to living a very generous lifestyle; all in a very short matter of time. I now had a big problem. I didn't know how to handle my new life. I didn't have the ability to manage my new found blessings. I couldn't keep up. Life was just happening too quickly for me. I was promoted to sales manager over the company. With my new promotion, my job quickly became my top priority. I wanted to prove to everyone that I was the best at what I do.

By working hard to be the best, I started to let pride creep into my life. I felt I was the best. Before long I had a big paycheck, nice car, new house, and everything I could possibly ever want. I didn't know pride always comes right before the fall. At the time, I felt I was the one who made my life's events happen. I felt I was indestructible and completely in control of my future. I thought that I made myself through hard work and determination. The truth is, God was pouring out his blessings on me and my family. Humbly I see now, it was all God.

With my new promotion there came more responsibilities, and I was starting to work my life away. I was off one day a week and usually got home around nine at night. My wife understood the long hours that I worked, as she was in retail too. I didn't know how to balance my work schedule and my family life together effectively. There just wasn't enough time for everything. Although we didn't discuss my working all the time, it was starting to affect our relationship. We didn't make time for each other like we should have done. With the daily grind of retail sales, we felt like our routine had come to a boiling point. It was time for a change.

9

Our New Beginning

In the next few months, the dealership experienced a lot of managerial changes. The general manager and finance director went to work at a dealership in Columbus Ohio. The finance director soon contacted me to let me know they needed a sales manager. He said it was a great opportunity for me to quickly advance in the company and make a lot of money. I won't lie, I was hesitant at first. I had never lived anywhere else before. Moving to Columbus would be a major transition for me and my wife. We were used to a small town atmosphere, and Columbus was a major city. This would be an enormous adjustment from our usual walk of life.

I was ready for a change. Our new general manager didn't have a clue on how to run a successful car dealership. The numbers were slipping because of his erroneous ways. It was like the corporate monkeys hired Homer Simpson to oversee the whole dealership. I remember thinking, "What did I do to deserve this punishment?" The new GM couldn't even turn on and use a computer. Our corporate office required reports to be done daily, so they could monitor our progress from another location. After several attempts from the new GM to open Microsoft Excel and create a report, he was unsuccessful. I inherited the responsibility. With a bewildered look on my face, I thought, "Where did they get this guy from? This is such a simple report to do. What will this joker do when I take a day off?" Now don't get me wrong, I'm sure that back in his day he was good at his job, but he was washed up and needed to be put out to pasture.

The new GM was from the old way of thinking when it came to car sales. He said I was too young to be a sales manager. He then told me I was the luckiest guy in the world and must have been in the right place at the right time. Naturally, this didn't set well with me. I was very proud of my accomplishments. I explained to him that it was hard work and determination that got me where I am today. I saw that it was just a matter of time before this powder keg exploded.

After much consideration, I ran the idea past my wife. I told her that I felt we were in a rut and needed some adventure in our lives. Moving could be a great opportunity for both of us. She agreed. My wife had been at her job for over six years and felt she was being overlooked for management positions. She received her degree in business management and wanted to find a career where she could use it. We discussed the pros and cons of making the move. After major consideration, we decided it would be best to move. I called my contact and got the process started. My wife made some phone calls too, and was able to transfer her job to a store there locally.

This was a huge decision to make in our lives. We knew we were both young with no real ties keeping us here. If it didn't work out, we could always move back. We made sure to leave on good terms just in case we needed to ask for our old jobs back. We thought that we planned everything out so carefully. We neglected to do one thing. We should've elected to take our decision to the Lord. This turned out to be a valuable lesson learned.

The first couple of months weren't bad. We had bought a new home. It was a beautiful brick rancher, single car garage, setting on .52 acres. It was equipped with two fireplaces and a pool table. Nestled in the heart of town, the house was hidden by a barrier of tall pine trees surrounding the perimeter. We were very fortunate to find privacy in a large city. We had plenty of grass to mow that's for sure. I always had a new company vehicle to drive. I made sure that she had a nice vehicle too. I was also making money hand over fist. We were in a position for the first time in our lives that money was no longer an issue.

We tried to find a suitable church while living in Columbus. The first church we visited must've had over one thousand people in attendance. They had three different schedules for Sunday morning service. This church was exactly what my wife was trying to avoid. She liked attending a small church. In her eyes, we attended the perfect church back home. She missed the little white church on the hillside. The pastor kept her attention there, as he had a way with words. To any believer, this was very important. He had a way of delivering his message across in a clear, meaningful, and understanding way. Trying to find a church she would be happy with soon found to be a challenge.

We found a church one day that was only a few miles away from where we lived. This church fit the description. We decided to go there the very next Sunday. The people seemed very friendly and greeted us with open arms. Once the service started, the preacher asked everyone to turn their Bibles to Matthew chapter three. We started to follow along as he read out load. All of a sudden our Bibles didn't match up. The preacher's Bible added words that mine did not have. I had read a little in the book of Revelation, where it says not to add or take away from the Word of God. I also remembered the other church that I attended that didn't preach the Word of God at all. I didn't feel comfortable sitting in a church that didn't use a King James Version of the Bible. At the time, I felt that the Bible they were preaching from was not the Word of God. How could it be? Their Bible added not just words but sentences that my Bible of course did not have. I was ready to leave. It upset me so much that we didn't return. We tried another church a little later on, but it just didn't feel right either. After three churches, my wife used the old baseball analogy, "Three strikes makes an out. It just wasn't meant to be."

I did pick up a new habit while in Columbus. I started praying at night. I really didn't know how to pray at the time, but I thought, "You have to start somewhere." I knew prayer was essentially just talking to God. I figured that I would start out small with my prayers and see how it goes.

I did pray occasionally from time to time, when I felt it was necessary. It seemed like previously in my life, it took a major incident like some illness or accident to get the prayer juices flowing. I felt that this act of disobedience had gone on long enough. My new prayers usually consisted of thanking God for His blessings and watching over my family. There were a lot of thank you prayers. I prayed nightly to watch over my mother, take care of her, and bring someone into her life that would make her happy. I prayed this routinely. I also said a prayer for my father. I didn't know much about him. Ultimately I wanted my mom and dad to somehow find each other again.

Once the freshness of our new lives wore off, things took a slight turn for the worse. My wife's Grandpa was involved in a machinery accident and he lost a finger. We were too wrapped up in our work schedules to go see him. Anytime our family got sick, it was the same thing. We both had grandparents that lived more than three hours away, and were getting along in age. We didn't contemplate about the little things like missing our family, before we decided to move to Columbus.

My wife wasn't very happy at her new job. Her boss was a young guy that thought it would be best for business to put down his employees all day and make their lives miserable. He was very immature and unprofessional when it came to work. She would come home most days distressed and agitated. I threatened numerous times to go and have a "talk" with him. We all knew that wouldn't end well. My wife didn't need to work, in the sense that we needed money. She's just one of those rare people, that being hard worker is built into their DNA. This trait is something I've always admired about her.

I was working more hours than ever before. I would have to attend a sales meeting at seven in the morning, and I would get home most nights around ten o'clock at night. I was happy with my job, but I was working my life away. I thought that working long hours was required to get ahead in life.

The owner of the dealership, who was seventy five, worked seven days a week till close. He micro managed everything. I remember him yelling at one of the employees for throwing away a two cent key tag that he made an error on. He was visibly upset when the salesman tossed it in the trash. "Kevin that was two cents of my money you just threw away. I outta deduct that from your paycheck." Our seven in the morning sales meeting usually consisted of the current market prices of fruit, buy one get one free suits on sale, and the reminiscing of the old days in the car business.

On New Year's Eve we had a daunting surprise. Someone tried to break into our home. Around midnight we heard a loud commotion coming from outside the garage. The only thing that kept them from entering was my dog's aggressive barking. Most likely young kids, these delinquents ransacked my wife's new SUV. They didn't steal anything, but created a huge mess. They scattered her belongings all over the back and side yards. I say they were probably young kids or teenagers, because the next morning I found out someone also toilet papered most of the trees in our front yard.

I've never faced this type of scenario before. Let's face it, I had a weak home defense system. Our last neighborhood didn't have a lot of break-ins. When we lived in our last house, we left the front door unlocked most of the time. My wife never locked the car doors. The crime of a big city never crossed my mind. I didn't own a gun and my state-of-the-art home security consisted of a shaggy dog and a baseball bat. I didn't like this unbridled feeling of not being in full control of the situation.

Being the man of the house, I had some decisions to make. First of all I installed a home security system. Then I started thinking, I work so many hours. What if my wife is home alone and someone breaks in. I couldn't live with the idea of something tragic happening to her. Once this thought entered my mind, it was like cancer. It was eating me up inside. There's no way my wife could fend off an attacker. I had to do something to protect her in case this happens again. Thankfully, I was at home during the last incident. Next time, I might not be so lucky.

My wife wasn't happy with her job and was at a crossroads. We discussed the possibility of her going back to school. She loved animals and had a special interest in becoming a veterinarian. She had checked into some classes, but that's as far as it went. I was so tired of seeing the tears roll down her cheeks as she told me about her day. She deserved better. Besides the boring morning meetings I was happy at my job, but I knew I could sell cars anywhere. The hours I put in each day were a bit much. I had developed a good reputation back in my home state and I knew it wouldn't be hard to find another job. Life hadn't turned out the way that we planned. I remembered my wife saying, "If it doesn't work out, we can always go back home." That started to sound better all the time.

I believe that God taught me a valuable lesson while living in Columbus. I came to the conclusion that money doesn't always equal happiness. My wife and I were in that rut again, but this time it was deeper than ever. I felt that for the first time in my life, I could be on the verge of losing it all if something didn't change. Moving to Columbus was a huge mistake. It was time to cut all ties. I made my decision; we were heading home.

10

Cause for Alarm

One night I had the worst dream possible. It took place only a few days before our move back home. When the dream started, everything was pitch-black. I couldn't see my hand in front of my face, and the air was dripping hot. I remember this dream vividly. With all the fine details, I felt completely immersed in this dream. You know how sometimes one can have a dream, and it is like a movie being played out in your mind? This phantasm was not the case. This illusion had every emotion attached to it. I felt every pain and anguish as my mind raced on.

In my dream, I immediately felt my body rooted and anchored, so that I couldn't move freely. It felt like my body was fixed with chains or couplings. I tried to sit, but the shackles were tightly secured from my hands to my ankles and wouldn't let me. I could hear the clinging of the chains as I struggled to get free. I remember thinking, "Where am I?"

A sinister feeling quickly touched me as I impatiently struggled to break free in the now shadowy darkness. The feelings that overcame me were jilted and forsaken; abandonment. I could hear a faint moaning in the distance, yet I could feel that I was alone. The feeling of solitude was so heavy that, it was in the air. I could taste the loneliness thick on my tongue when I opened my mouth. This feeling of solitude now quivered through my whole body. I could hear agony starting to build all around me. I moved to try and get free, but my body wouldn't respond to its commands. Was I in shock, or was this paralyzing fear? I managed to strike my wrists together forcefully, and a spark shot out. For a split second I could see my surroundings.

There were grotesque-looking beast's great and small, staring at me from a distance. These wild-eyed creatures were also bound and chained in shackles. I felt like these monsters were peering through my soul. I was in a place of torments. I could see water dripping like ice from the ceiling. When the water hit the ground, it dissipated into steam from the floor's heat. It sounded like someone had snuffed out a flame.

Once the spark relinquished, I could see only darkness. I knew exactly where I was. Somehow, someway; I was in Hell. Hades. My emotions now fluttered erratically like a butterfly trying to escape a spider's web. I could feel the panic starting to race through my veins now. Frantically I screamed, "No, no. NO!"

I clattered my chains together again to get another look around. As a spark came out, I could see to the left of me giant animal-like monsters chained up against a wall. Again, they were watching me intently. "How did I get here? More importantly, how do I get out of here?" I was sweating from the heat that was coming off the sides of the walls. I could feel hot ashes in between my toes when I moved my feet around. I didn't understand why I was here. This feeling of abandonment hurt the most. I screamed loudly, "I'm saved. I do not belong here. I need help. Somebody, help me!"

There was another barbarous creature to the right of me who started to bang on an anvil. This animal was quite a spectacle. The monster was tall and muscular, and had a head like a bull. He was crimson red, with coloring like blood. With just a few seconds of light from the strikes, I could see by his forehead brow he wasn't playing around. The beast fervently banged the anvil now. The sparks would light the room every time he hit the anvil. I could now smell a burnt savor like brimstone, searing all around me. I wasn't sure what his motives were, but he was working purposely to finish the job.

I now focused sharply on the anvil as sparks were increasingly streaming. Clang clank, clang clank. Clang clank. I listened intently as everything suddenly went grimly silent. The creature had come to a grinding halt. A cold chill suddenly grasped the air. The beast let go a screeching moan and hammered the anvil one last time.

With one last strike of the anvil, I suddenly awoke from this hellish nightmare. I gained consciousness and speedily scrambled for any kind of light. My eyes fixated on the alarm clock that was positioned on a corner table. As I set up in bed and looked around, I remember thinking, "It all felt so real." I laid my head back down on my pillow, and meditated a bit on my dream. "Was this God trying to tell me something?" I tried to shrug that thought off, but it kept coming back. "If so, what was it? What are You trying to tell me?" I was too haughty to admit to the Lord that I needed to change. I wrangled with these thoughts for a while longer, but eventually closed my eyes for the rest of the night.

As I am writing about my dream, I want to stop and thank You Lord for my second chance at life. "Dear Lord, I just want to thank You for allowing me to change my ways. I know now that I was arrogant and high-minded, yet You looked past that and loved me anyways. I see now that I was a fool and ignored You're warnings so many times. When You tried to reach out, I was too irrational to listen. Although I had good intentions, I was too busy with my life to hear You. Thank You for knowing my heart and seeing the good in me. I put You second in my life Lord and I am truly sorry for this. Forgive me Lord, I hear You clearly now. Walk beside me Lord in my life's journey. Guide me along the right path. I want to thank You Lord, for my second chance to know and follow You. In Jesus name I pray this. Amen."

11

What about Hell?

In 2013, the True Life in God Foundation surveyed Americans on the question: Do Americans believe in Heaven and Hell? The results were pretty impressive. According to the survey, 62% of Americans believe in Heaven and think they are going there one day. The survey also showed us that 56% of Americans believe in the devil and 53% believe in Hell. Only 44% believed that Hell is a place of suffering and punishment people go to after they die. So then, what exactly is Hell? If over half the people in America believe there is a Hell, what do they really know about it? Here's just a glimpse of what the Scripture says about this fiery inferno.

Did you know that even the atheist will one day believe in Jesus? Unfortunately it will be too late for them. Philippians 2:10-11 says: *That at the name of Jesus every knee should bow, of things in heaven, and things in earth, and things under the earth; And that every tongue should confess that Jesus Christ is Lord, to the glory of God the Father.* Hell unfortunately will be filled with the nonbeliever. They will spend an eternity removed from God. Revelation 20:15 says: *And if anyone's name was not found written in the book of life, he was thrown into the lake of fire.* Simply put, if you do not believe in Jesus as your Savior, you are headed for Hell.

    We previously discussed Heaven as a place God has created for all of his followers. God has created a place for the doubter too. Hell is described in the Bible as a place where you are eternally separated from God. There will be no parties in Hell. It is a place of physical agony, mental suffering, loneliness, and emotional sorrow. Hell was created by God for the devil and his demons. Matthew 25:41. The Bible illustrates Hell as a bottomless pit. It also depicts Hell as the weeping and gnashing of teeth. An unquenchable thirst. Matthew 5:30 tells us: *And if thy right hand offend thee, cut it off, and cast it from thee: for it is profitable for thee that one of thy members should perish, and not that thy whole body should be cast into hell.* Revelation 14:11 describes Hell as a constant torment day and night. The pain is never ceasing torments for eternity; all for not accepting Jesus as Savior.

    Throughout creation, man has made excuses on why not to accept Jesus as Lord. One excuse is that they don't have time in their life for God, or the time is not right. This excuse is becoming more common among the masses. Life seems busier now then it was even a hundred years ago, yet this is no excuse on why the world's population can't spend time with God. Everyone has twenty four hours in a day, how do *you* use them?

Our Heavenly Father wants us to spend our time wisely. Minutes turn into hours, which turn into days, months, and before too long years. Before you know it, our time is up. God wants us to spend our time communing with Him. I spend my time in fellowship with God on a daily basis. I enjoy spending my time with the Lord, even if it's just to say thank you for His blessings. When I awake I usually read His Word. On my way to work I listen to His Word an audio book and meditate in the moment. I walk with Him daily and discuss everything that's happening in my life. By doing this, the Lord guides and shows me the right decision to make in that particular situation. You can have a deep, personal, and intimate relationship with the Lord too.

There are young people today, who believe "I'll just wait till I'm older to accept God." The problem with this statement is that you might not have the chance to. There are people that die every day from unexpected sickness and accidents.

God is omniscient and knows everything: past, present, and future. The Bible tells us this in 1 John 3:20. God, who is the Creator of the Heavens and earth, says that the very hairs on your head are all numbered. He knows what will happen tomorrow and forever. He knows your friends and your enemies. He also knows the condition of your heart, and how deep you are in sin. Since He is omniscient, He has the power to change anything and everything in your life at any given moment. Only He knows when you will draw your last breath, so do not delay in your decision to accept Jesus. Many have waited until it's too late. Every day you procrastinate, you are missing out on the immeasurable and unconditional love our Savior has waiting for you.

In the book of Luke, Jesus tells us a parable of a rich fool that decides to tear down his barns and build bigger ones. God said to him, "Thou fool, this night thy soul shall be required of thee." The Bible teaches us that today is the day of salvation. I strongly urge you: Do not put this vocation aside for another day. Nothing has to stand in the way of you doing business with the Lord. By dragging your feet, you miss out on God's abundance and fullness that He has planned for you.

There are many people that think they need to "see" before they believe. The Bible tells us in 2 Corinthians 5:7: *For we walk by faith, not by sight.* Faith is having trust in God's Word. Having assurance in knowing that God will do the right thing in your life, as He guides you through life's venture, is faith. In Hebrews 11:1 Paul describes faith: *Now faith is the substance of things hoped for, the evidence of things not seen.* In John 20:29, Jesus makes a powerful statement about faith: *Jesus saith unto him, Thomas, because thou hast seen me, thou hast believed: blessed are they that have not seen, and yet have believed.* Romans 10:17 tells us faith comes from hearing God's Word. Since God is omniscient; having faith in Him and the Word He gave us, only makes sense. He is the Creator of the universe and everything in it. God knows the past, present, and the future. Won't you put your faith in Him?

Finally, there are people that will never put their trust in God. While God offers this free gift or salvation to everyone, there are still people that refuse Him. Psalms 14:1 tells us: *The fool hath said in his heart, There is no God. They are corrupt, they have done abominable works, there is none that doeth good.* You might know someone who is relentless and stubborn, that won't accept Jesus as Lord and Savior. Don't give up hope. The Bible teaches us to pray for those who are lost. *To open their eyes, so that they may turn from darkness to light and from the power of Satan to God, that they may receive forgiveness of sins and a place among those who are sanctified by faith in me.* Acts 26:18.

I once worked with a man that I admired as a coworker. He was honest, hardworking, and someone we looked up to. He was someone I could count on at work to do the right thing. One day we had a conversation about God. I was able to witness to him about Jesus. After I had finished talking, he told me a story on how his mother and sister were always hounding him about getting saved. At this point his emotions changed. I could see that there was a lot of pressure coming from his family. I asked if there is something that he didn't understand that I could help him with. He started to shut down on me and the conversation. With a defensive demeanor he said, "Look, I believe that Jesus existed. I guess He was a good man, but just a man like you and me. Jesus Christ wasn't the Son of God." My jaw dropped to the floor. This was very strong ideology coming from someone that I considered an ally. I knew that God was dealing with his heart. I could hear the self-doubt in his voice. He went on to say that Jesus was like a super hero in everyone's history books, but he didn't believe that Jesus did any real miracles. I didn't put any pressure on him. I simply said, "I am here if you want to talk about it."

My co-worker, who was in his fifties, had made up some crazy story about Jesus that he believed was true. He didn't want to face the truth. My friend was listening to the devil's lies that filled his head. He was blinded, stubborn, and refused to listen to the truth that was presented before him. I continued to talk to him about the Gospel over the next few years. Sometimes he'd listen sometimes he wouldn't. This man had missed the mark. I know he heard the Gospel, yet he didn't want to accept it. I told him that he can be saved anywhere at any time. I even offered to walk him through the prayer if need be. He later changed jobs and we lost touch with one another. I pray that he gets saved before his time is up. Once it's too late, there is no second chance. The Bible teaches us that anyone that does not abide in God's Word is destined for Hell.

God does not want anyone to spend eternity in Hell. He has given every man the choice of where he will spend eternity. God will not force you to believe one way or the other. He will simply present the truth to you in His own way. It's up to you to decide. Whether it is delivered through a book, the radio, or person to person, God will get the Gospel to you. Romans 1:20 says that we are without excuse if we do not accept Him. God will give everyone the opportunity to follow Him. The gift of Christ is there for you. Will you have faith in Him?

12

Storm Watch

He stilled the storm to a whisper; the waves of the sea were hushed. They were glad when it grew calm, and he guided them to their desired haven.
Psalm 107:29-30 (NIV)

It was an exciting time in our lives. My wife and I decided we had enough of the strenuous life and big city lights, so we headed back to the simple life of the country. She is a country girl at heart, so what would be better than to find our little slice of Heaven out in the sticks. We found a beautiful four bedroom rancher with a two car garage, seated on thirteen acres. The terrain was mostly rolling hills, and it had almost six acres of flat land to mow, garden, and maintain. It came with enough flat land to build the barn my wife had been wanting. Our new house set privately on a mountaintop, so much so that our closest neighbors lived about a half a mile away. This property was the perfect farmland we had always dreamed of. This land was everything that I've ever wanted: A nice house, acreage, two ponds, and a ton of room to expand on.

Today started off exceptionally well, with springtime clearly in the air. You could hear a whippoorwill off in the distance, singing his love song to anyone that would listen. Wild daisies and honeysuckle were blooming carelessly on the hillside. Earlier that morning we watched a young white-tailed deer standing in the front yard feasting on wild clover. Everything felt so fresh and new. We moved in only a few days before, but this was the first day that we would be able to enjoy working on the farm. I did not know that today's events, which were rapidly unravelling, would forever change the lives of everyone involved. I had no idea a storm was slowly brewing in the shadows.

My mother decided to visit us and help my wife with painting and rearranging, while I handled all of the outside chores. The previous owners had very bad taste in interior decorating. They had a bubble gum pink bedroom with a pink border, fixed up for their young daughter. The living room was painted a very tacky dark blue. They also had a bedroom painted red, blue, and yellow. It reminded you of a McDonald's play land. The colors were so frumpy that every room needed repainted. They previous owners also installed a shoddy book shelf, covering one half of the living room wall. The shelving would soon be removed.

My wife was supposed to go to a horse show in Tennessee, but decided to cancel last minute because there was just too much work to do on the house. I called a few days earlier and had the water and electricity turned on. We still needed to hookup the phone, internet, and cable. Our cell phone reception at the house was spotty at best. If one stood out in the driveway on a clear day, one might get enough signal to make a call. Most of the time the call was disconnected before it was completed.

The house had been on the market for a few months now, and the grass was so high that it would be impossible to cut with a push mower. I decided before I mow, I should first survey the land we bought. I neglected to walk the property lines before we bought our house. The day we came to look at the property, it snowed several inches. We liked what we did see of the property so much that we pulled the trigger and bought it without viewing the rest of the rocky terrain.

I recently purchased an ATV 4wd so I could easily navigate all of the property that we had just purchased. This four wheeler was definitely more ATV then I needed, but it was such a great deal I couldn't resist. I made a quick loop and surveyed the land. It looked like the grass hadn't been cut at all this year. The property definitely needs a brush hog brought in to cut out some or the debris. The growth of weeds and shrubs had grown out of control.

After devising a plan, I made my way back to the garage to get started. The riding lawnmower had plenty of gas, so I fired it up and began cutting. The grass was still wet from the morning dew and that made it hard for the lawnmower to mulch and dispense. The front yard was over an acre, with lots of trees and bushes to cut around. This took about an hour to complete. Once I finished with the front and back yards, I cut my way around the pond and to the back of the property.

This area of grass had extremely rough terrain. There were a lot of uneven slopes and hillsides. I rode up to the patchy turf of grass on my riding lawnmower, to observe just how rough the terrain was. The midday sun was now beating down on my brow. I looked left then right, wondering if I should attempt to cut the grass with the push or riding mower. While parked on the hill's edge, my riding lawn mower stopped running. After several attempts to restart it, I decided it must be out of gas. I was surprised that it made it this long without needing to refuel. It had been several hours since I first started mowing. I did not know this was the beginning of God's miracle.

I ran out of gas right on the edge of an embankment. I looked around and saw that I was several acres away from the house. It would be easier to grab the gas can and refuel the mower right on the ledge. I set the parking brake and dismounted from the mower. As soon as I stood up, the lawnmower spontaneously thrust down the hillside and crashed into a tree. I just stood there for a moment in bewilderment. I peered down the hill at the sudden impact. After reflecting for a moment on the crash, I remember thinking, "I set the parking brake. How did this happen?"

I scrambled down the hill to survey the damage. The lawnmower slammed up against a tall birch tree. The force put a huge dent in the front of the hood and damaged the starting gears of the lawnmower. The sudden velocity penned the mower up against the tree, so that I couldn't push it free. I tried starting it, but remembered it was out of gas. The starter was dragging and made a grinding sound when it turned over. "Great." Everything was going smoothly up to this point. I didn't need a distraction like this to slow down my workday.

I made my way back to the house and went inside for a drink of water. I can't believe this happened. I set the parking brake and it still shot down the hill and crashed into a tree. How was I going to get that lawnmower up the steep incline when it doesn't even run? My wife asked me what I was working on. I knew if I told her the truth, she wouldn't like it much. I finished my drink of water and told her I was "fishing out a lawnmower" as I ran out the door.

I gathered a tow strap and headed back out to the crash site on my ATV. This area was shaded by trees, and the grass was still wet from the morning dew. I turned wide and slowly crept down the hill. After I made it to the bottom where the crash site was, I turned the ATV off and began hooking up the tow strap. I securely tightened the strap around the hitch of the ATV to the lawnmower. "Here goes nothing." I gave the ATV some gas and it began spinning in the slippery grass.

As I backed down the hill to get another run at it, I looked to the side and seen that my wheel was just inches away from dropping off a rather large cliff and falling into a ravine. The roots from another tree were unraveled and spreading off the cliff's edge. There were globs of dirt breaking away from the tree's blackened roots. I remember thinking, "I better not back up and hit that drop off." I locked my ATV in four wheel drive and gave the throttle some gas.

After a few moments, I opened my swollen eyes as instinct frantically took over. My eyes were filled with a gooey substance obstructing my vision. I didn't know where I was or what had transpired. I desperately felt around for anything I could grasp onto. My fingernails dug deep into the earth's soil as I began to crawl my way to the top of the hill. My body was reacting to the situation as adrenaline pumped through my veins. I thought, "Why can't I see anything?" I kept clawing and scratching as I seemed like I was making progress. I felt a burning sensation when I touched my right leg, as I continued to crawl up the steep rocky ridge.

I scurried to the top of the hill and wiped the dirt and debris from my eyes. This took a moment as my whole body was covered in dead leaves, dirt, and mud. I could hear a faint vibration thumping in both ears; whooshing like that of an ocean tide whirling against a broken shore. As I wiped the cold sweat from my brow, I noticed that I had blood in between the webbing of my right hand. I tried wiping it on my shorts but I realized that they were too the color of blood. "What's going on? I must be hurt." The throbbing pain in my leg was now growing stronger. That must be where the blood was coming from. I glared across multiple acres to my house and back again. My mind told me that I must be hurt although I didn't feel very much pain other than the cut on my leg. The scorching heat had dried my mouth. My face was covered with dirt and fragments of leaves, which also covered the outside of my quivering lips.

With the whooshing sound now throbbing in the back of my head, I decided to make my way back to the house. I stammered past the pond about an acre and then stopped. "Maybe my wife can pour me a glass of water. Why is it so hot out here? I only have a few more steps to go. Why am I so tired?" I suddenly had a multitude of thoughts racing through my head, perhaps too many. I pressed on but stumbled a little, now dragging both feet on the gravel surface. "A few more feet and I can sit down. My body felt faint as I pushed myself forward.

I made my way through the garage and opened the door to the living room. My mother screamed frantically in terror and disbelief. My wife had a panic look on her face and rushed over to access the situation. My mother told her to get help. I looked through the window and saw my wife driving off in her SUV with dust burning up the driveway. I made it to the sofa and set down. My mother held my head gently and applied pressure to the right side. "What's wrong?" I started to feel concerned. It worried me that my mother wasn't answering my questions. She asked if I had a cell phone. I told her it was on the kitchen counter but it probably wouldn't work because of a weak signal. I kept asking her, "What's wrong. What's wrong?" I could see the fear whelming up in her eyes. I asked her again, "What's wrong?" This time my speech slurred a bit. I asked the same question again. "Wh-at's wr-ong with me?" My mother handed me the cell phone and asked if I could dial 911. I did so and to my surprise I heard the operator say, "This is 911, what's your emergency?" I handed the phone over to her as I slowly faded away.

13

Trials and Tribulations

My Sunday school teacher once said, "It seems like we are either always moving into a storm, in the middle of a storm, or exiting a storm." I really didn't take much thought of this until recently. God has been so good to me. He carried me through a tremendous personal storm. By the grace of God, I am still walking on this earth. I know that God has a purpose for me. I trust in Him and know that He has work for me still. *For I know the thoughts that I think toward you, saith the LORD, thoughts of peace, and not of evil, to give you an expected end.* Jeremiah 29:11.

A difficult part of being a Christian is that we are not immune to life's hardships. The Bible tells us that everyone will experience trials in their life. *That ye may be the children of your Father which is in heaven: for he maketh his sun to rise on the evil and on the good, and sendeth rain on the just and on the unjust.* Matthew 5:45. When God sends a storm our way, He doesn't do it to try and sink us, but to help develop us. God sends these trials to help us grow in our spiritual walk. His goal is to have us walk closer with Him.

For me, I was a slothful Christian. I didn't know how to mature and grow in Christ. I finally decided to just "believe and let it be." Thankfully, God had other plans. He tried subtle ways at first to get my attention, but I ignored God every time He called out to me. Restlessness and some intimate failures first come to mind when I now look back. He had also tried to obtain my attention through several blessings, but again I turned a deaf ear. If it wasn't for God giving me a great "wake up call", I might never have witnessed the glorious blessings He had in store for me. It took a life threatening experience before I started to listen to God.

Everyone's heard the expression, "What doesn't kill you makes you stronger." For me, there is some truth to this saying. When my life almost came to an end, I trusted fully in God and He carried me through. Not only was I facing a physical trial but a spiritual one as well. God healed and renewed me: Body, mind, and spirit.

Trials can affect our lives in many different ways. A trial could come in the form of a sudden change in jobs, death of a child, sickness, or in my case an accident. Whatever the storm may be that you are facing, don't give up hope. Talk to God and He will show you the way. *Rejoice in hope, be patient in tribulation, be constant in prayer.* Romans 12:12.

Our Heavenly Father will not permit a trial or temptation to happen that we cannot handle. 1

Corinthians 10:13 tells us: *There hath no temptation taken you but such as is common to man: but God is faithful, who will not suffer you to be tempted above that ye are able; but will with the temptation also make a way to escape, that ye may be able to bear it.* When we endure our trials and overcome temptation, God tells us we will receive the crown of life. James 1:12 says: *Blessed is the man that endureth temptation: for when he is tried, he shall receive the crown of life, which the Lord hath promised to them that love him.* Trials are presented in life to shape our Godly character. Our sufferings bring us perseverance and hope. When we have affliction and adversity in our lives, look to the Lord for the strength to overcome it. *I can do all things through him who strengthens me.* Philippians 4:13.

God tells us in Hebrews 13:5 that He will never leave us or forsake us. God will be with us right up until to the very end. No matter how heavy a burden our affliction is, God is there. He wants you to call upon Him, and He will comfort you. In Matthew 28:11 it says: *Come unto me, all ye that labour and are heavy laden, and I will give you rest.*

God permits trials in our lives, but He doesn't always initiate them. The source of all life's burdens is created by either yourself, God, or the devil. If we are troubled by storms of the devil, I assure you that God is part of and is engineering the end of all our tribulations. All things work together for good to them that love God. He gives us this promise in Romans 8:28.

All Christians will face persecution. Scripture tells us this in Timothy 3:12. *Yea, and all that will live godly in Christ Jesus shall suffer persecution.* Christians are persecuted because their belief in Jesus Christ as Savior does not conform to the godlessness of our sinful world. The devil can physically attack us with illness, disasters, and persecution. He uses "spiritual terrorist attacks" to try and somehow weaken our faith in God. God tells us to be constantly on our toes because the devil will tempt us during persecution. The Bible tells us in 1 Peter 5:8-9: *Be sober, be vigilant; because your adversary the devil, as a roaring lion, walketh about, seeking whom he may devour: Whom resist stedfast in the faith, knowing that the same afflictions are accomplished in your brethren that are in the world.* We must be ready every time the enemy advances. When a Christian is being persecuted, we must stay vigilant and sharp, especially when the lion is on the prowl.

When you are faced with a storm, the devil will try his hardest to discourage you. The voice in your head might tell you that you are worthless, and that you are to blame for the affliction. This is not the case. The devil wants to bring you down anyway he can. He is also good at bringing up "old sins." The devil wants you to dwell on your past transgressions. God on the other hand, is faithful and just to forgive us of our sins. If you pray and ask for clemency, the Bible teaches us that God will cast your sins as far as the east is from the west.

God instructs us in His Scripture on how to defeat the enemy. In Psalms 23 God tells us to fear no evil. Ephesians 6 urges us to put on the full armor of God; then we can defeat the wiles of the Devil. Do not let Satan attack you during these trials. The devil wants us to be tempted, and then condemns us all at the same time. Don't worry my friend. God tells us in 1 Corinthians 10:13: *There hath no temptation taken you but such as is common to man: but God is faithful, who will not suffer you to be tempted above that ye are able; but will with the temptation also make a way to escape, that ye may be able to bear it.* Rely on God for your strength. He will carry you through life's fiercest storms.

Be assured that God uses our trials to one day become a blessing. We might not understand right away why God permits certain things to happen, but be assured God works for the good of us. In 2 Corinthians 4 16:18, God explains this to us: *For which cause we faint not; but though our outward man perish, yet the inward man is renewed day by day. For our light affliction, which is but for a moment, worketh for us a far more exceeding and eternal weight of glory; While we look not at the things which are seen, but at the things which are not seen: for the things which are seen are temporal; but the things which are not seen are eternal.* This has come true for me in so many ways. I didn't understand at the time why I had to go through such an affliction, yet because I trusted in Him, I have been blessed abundantly.

In Romans 8:28 God tells us that He works for the good of those who love Him, who have been called according to His purpose. Sometimes even the smallest trials in our lives can result in enormous blessings. One of our elder pastors at church hit a large pot hole the other day and it flattened his passenger front tire. He called a fellow brother in Christ to come help him with the tire change. While waiting for the friend's arrival, he asked the Lord, "Why did you let this happen to me? Why have you given me this burden to deal with?" The friend soon arrived and replaced the flattened tire with a donut tire so he could get to a repair shop. Once he arrived at the garage, the mechanics did their inspection which led to an alarming discovery. The drivers-side front tire's tread had been severely damaged on the inside of the tire. No one would have noticed this without taking the tire off. The tread belts had worn through the tire and could have punctured at any time. The pastor then remembered asking God, "why Lord why" as he thanked Him for his misfortune. This trial became a blessing from God and possibly saved him from a future accident.

God has taken me, and brought me through a mighty storm. I once was a lukewarm Christian, but now by the mercy of God, I walk with Him. The Bible teaches us not to be taken aback by the trials we go through. Instead, be delighted in the fact that Christ loves us and walks with us right to the very end. 1 Peter 4:12-13 reads: *Dear friends, don't be surprised at the fiery trials you are going through, as if something strange were happening to you. Instead, be very glad—for these trials make you partners with Christ in his suffering, so that you will have the wonderful joy of seeing his glory when it is revealed to all the world.*

I am not afraid. The trials that I endure, strengthens my relationship with the Lord. If you trust in the Lord, your trials will make you stronger. We learn to be a better Christian, walk closer with the Lord, and submit to His will with every trial that we sustain. Trust in the Lord with all your trials and remember this: At the end of every storm, there is the Son who always shines.

14

Only God Knows

But I have spared you for a purpose—to show you my power and to spread my fame throughout the earth.
Exodus 9:16 New Living Translation (NLT)

For the next five days, only God knew what my future would hold. After I made the call to 911, help quickly arrived and I was transported to the local hospital. After the doctors did their examination, they broke the grim news to my wife. The diagnosis: two large skull fractures. A skull fracture is a break in one or more of the eight bones that form the cranial portion of the skull, usually occurring as a result of blunt force trauma. Lucky me. I lost a lot of blood, which was beginning to clot in my head. The doctors declared after examining the x rays, I had an epidural hematoma, or a blood clot, which was pressing against my brain. This new development was very dangerous and potentially deadly without immediate surgery.

I do not remember anything that occurred after I handed my mother the cell phone and dialed 911. Later on, my wife told me that I stayed conscious the whole time, right up until the surgery was performed. She said when the EMT's arrived at my house, my body was going into shock and I vomited while they were loading me onto a gurney. My mother rushed to my grandmother's house to pick her up and they quickly headed to the hospital. My wife rode with me in the ambulance to keep me company as the EMT's made sure I stayed with them.

The emergency surgery lasted almost eight hours. I was put into a medically induced coma after the procedure, to give my body time to heal. After the surgery was complete, the doctors did not give any good news. My wife was informed that if I woke up from the coma, I could be in a vegetative state for the rest of my life. The doctors were not sure that I would ever regain consciousness after the surgery. They also said that if I did recover, I could be limited in my abilities. Naturally this was not what my family wanted to hear. My wife was heartbroken over the fact that she could still lose me. The doctors explained that my body needs time to heel from the injury, and they do not know how much damage was done to the brain during the accident. They basically said it's a "wait and see what happens" situation.

While the doctors performed their best Hail Mary, the next five days would be filled with grief, worry, and fear for my family. The doctors did not paint a good picture. In all likelihood, the future did not look good for me. I had family from Wisconsin, Texas, Ohio, Kentucky, and West

Virginia start to make their way to the hospital. My mother called my father and he too made the journey.

A mass prayer took place over the next few days. My mother and father n law had the pastor from their church come to the hospital and pray with my family. A deacon from the small church on the hill also visited. There was an enormous prayer chain that went out from all over, with people praying for my recovery. Many friends and family were there for my wife, giving her comfort and support during this difficult period of time. The doctors did their very best and now it was up to the Lord to decide if I lived or died. Thankfully, He heard everyone's prayers.

I know I didn't deserve a second chance. I ignored God on so many occasions. I could have done more. I could have spent more time in His Word, drawing closer to Him. Instead, I was too involved in my worldly plans to let Him in. I was too busy making a name for myself and taking care of my family to fellowship with God. I don't even want to think about what would've happened that day if God wasn't watching over me. Jesus carried me through the accident and my surgery. I look back now and see that I wasn't spiritually ready to meet the Lord. I still had a childish mentality when it came to my faith. I believed in God yet lacked any personal relationship. It took a major accident like this one to break the barriers down in my heart.

God showed me wonderful mercy. He spared my life and allowed time for a second attempt to make things right. I was too stubborn to hear Him calling, yet He loved me anyways. God blessed me with a second chance to know Him as my Savior. God has a plan for me and He has my attention.

15

Awake

*Show me the right path, O LORD;
point out the road for me to follow.
Lead me by your truth and teach me,
for you are the God who saves me.
All day long I put my hope in you.* **Psalms 25:4-5 (NLT)**

We all travel down life's winding road. For some that road stretches on for many years. For others, the journey only lasts a short distance. While we travel, we stumble across obstacles. Sometimes life's journey leads us down a road that's harsh and bumpy. Other times the path set before us is clear as far as the eye can see. At some point in our travel, we all reach a crossroad. When we arrive at the crossroads, we must decide on which direction to follow. Left will send us down a path of uncertainty. The right will lead us down the path to righteousness. I made it to the crossroad. I needed to decide right then and there if I was going to listen to God or keep ignoring Him. It was time to decide if I was going to put God first or keep Him last. God saw the good in me. He examined my heart and spared my life. Like every sinner, I had stumbled down the wrong path. God gave me a second chance to pick the right road. I needed to decide which way to go: left or right.

For the last five days I had been in a coma. Lying in the hospital bed my body lay frail and broken. While in ICU, my mother first noticed my subtle body movements. My wife was holding one hand and my mother held onto the other. While holding my hand, she felt a twitch. With a joyous tone she said, "He moved his hand, he moved his hand." I was tottering in and out of consciousness for a long while. Several hours later I finally awoke, singing an oldies song, "One is the loneliest number." This didn't seem unusual on my end, as I was always doing something that involved music. It took several days before I actually came too, falling in and out of a deep sleep. My body had taken a major blow and was now starting to heal.

I did manage to keep the nurses busy, breaking the wrists restraints on more than one occasion. Dazing in and out, I kept trying to pull on my intravenous tubes. I didn't know where I was or what was going on, when I broke the restraints. Once they moved me from ICU to a regular room, I was put into a restraint vest. One night I almost had the restraint vest off when my wife walked in the room. I had twisted my arm behind my back with some kind of contortionist move, and was almost freed. I grinned at my wife and said, "I almost had it."

Everyone was ecstatic to know that I was coming out of the coma. My wife was overcome with joy. The good Lord had heard the prayers to save me and spare my life. Now as I regained consciousness, the question was: Would I ever be the same?

The doctors did their evaluation now that the surgery was complete. I was dealing with some major pain. They were giving me morphine intravenously for the pain. Once the morphine was injected into my veins, I felt instant relief. The part of my brain that controls eyesight was severely damaged because of the accident. When I came to, I had blurred vision. As I looked around the room, everything I saw was fuzzy. My field of vision was damaged. I also had double vision. When I looked around things like the chair, people, even the clock on the wall looked like it was layered. I saw two of everything. The vision in my left eye was damaged the most. I had no peripheral vision in my left eye; I could only see straight ahead. My side vision was completely gone in my left eye.

I also acquired other disheartening new disabilities because of the accident. My head and brain were extremely swollen and I was in a lot of pain. My eyes were also swollen almost shut due to my injury. I had several hundred staples holding my skull in place. The swelling in my brain caused a lot of problems with my body not functioning properly. The left side of my body was mostly paralyzed. I couldn't stand or walk. I had only a little arm and hand movement at first. It was almost like I had a stroke with one half of my body being affected as a result. My memory was all but gone, and my short term memory was affected. I didn't know anything or anyone at first. My speech was affected as well. I developed a stutter.

I asked my wife what happened. She told me I was in an accident but I'm okay now. That's all I needed to know at the time. The road ahead of me would be a long one. Even though my body suffered greatly, I knew I was not alone. I remember making the statement to my family that God truly blessed me and allowed me to wake up from this horrible accident.

I had family from Texas and Wisconsin arrive about the same time. These were all cousins that I had grown up with. They were more like brothers and a sister to me. With my mind still very foggy, I remember waking up and seeing one of my cousins knelt there by my bedside. I saw that he was fighting back tears. This was a great man of stature, whom I greatly admired. I could see that he was in a lot of pain. The memory of him hurting so much will always be engraved in my mind. I didn't understand why he was so upset. My mind couldn't comprehend it. I remember feeling extremely stressed out, seeing him in such agony.

My cousin from Wisconsin had also arrived. He was my best friend when I was a child. We had some crazy adventures together, and were always in some kind of mischief together; like boys do. In our teen years, we decided to form a country band. There had been some bad blood between us when the band broke up, therefore leaving our relationship strained. Ten years had passed since I last saw him. When he entered the room, I remember bursting out in tears and he did too. We didn't have to say anything at all. As we cried together, everything was forgiven.

After a few days an occupational health therapist came into my room to aid with my recovery. This was the first time since my accident that I had experienced any kind of therapy. At first, the nurse seemed very friendly. She began to ask me a series of questions that I did not understand. Although they were simple questions, I did not know the answers. I had no memory of the past. I did not know my own name. I didn't know my own wife or most of my family. The therapist pushed me too hard, and so I began to shut down. She pressed on, "What day is it? Is it daylight or dark? Who is the President of the United States? What's your address? Where do you live? Do you even know your own name?" She was putting these questions in front of me before I even had time to think about the answer. I began to tell her, "I don't know, I don't know." Some of the answers I did know but I was done with her. She embarrassed me to the point that I was about to explode. I finally looked at her and said, "I guess that I'm just stupid." That was enough for my mother to step in and escort the lady into the hallway. As she had a few words with her, I began to cry. I didn't know most of the answers. I felt so ashamed. I thought, "What has happened to me? Why could I not comprehend those questions?" For the first time since I woke up, I felt very alone. I've always considered myself a smart person, but now I didn't know my own name? I humbly cried myself to sleep.

My wife was unprepared to deal with such a catastrophe. I was in control of the checkbook and handled everything financially. I handled the mortgage and car payments. She would now have to step in and manage the household. I just quit the dealership in Columbus a few days before my accident. I luckily signed the Cobra waiver on my way out. The Cobra form allows an employee so many days to continue insurance coverage after parting ways with the employer. Time was about to expire. We needed to get a check to the insurance company quickly. The dealership I worked for, went out of their way to help. My wife overnighted a check to the dealer to cover the insurance premiums. They rushed the paperwork to the insurance company just in the nick of time, allowing me to have insurance coverage.

I noticed that the foods that I once loved now tasted different from what I remembered. I guess my taste buds were as confused as I was. I begged and pleaded for a Pepsi. Pepsi was my number one choice of beverages. I loved the sweet taste of Pepsi. Once I finally acquired a Pepsi, it tasted horrible. It tasted very strong and acidity to me. I took a sip and set it down. I couldn't stand the flavor. None of the foods tasted like I remembered it. I had to relearn a lot of things, one being my food tastes.

The next day I had a new occupational health therapist. She first asked me to draw a house. I thought this would be easy. I found out quickly that it was not. My motor skills were severely damaged due to the accident. I could see the house that I wanted to draw in my mind, I just couldn't get my hand to cooperate. I drew a half square that took up the whole page. I asked for another piece of paper so I could try again. The result was much the same as I just couldn't make my drawing resemble anything like a house.

She said next we were going to try some math problems. "Let's start out with something easy. She gave me some simple plus and minus equations. I had no problem coming up with the right answers. As the problems grew harder, she pulled a calculator out and began entering in the equations. I answered a few problems faster than she could input them into her calculator. She asked my wife, "Has he always been this good at math?" We both turned and looked at each other. My wife replied, "His job requires to be fast at solving equations, but not that fast." She ran and got a doctor. She said to the doctor, "Watch this." She verbally gave me the equation. As she was entering it into her calculator, I said the answer before she could finish. The doctor turned to me, "Mr. Cooper, you are in stage three of your recovery. There are eight stages to someone recovering from a head trauma. Stage three is the autistic stage of a head injury. That usually involves some aggressive behavior." He turned to my wife and asked if I have showed any aggressive behavior towards anyone. She said no, nothing at all. He then changed his mind and said that I might be in between stage three and four right now. The therapist then said that was the end of our session. I was extremely tired and quickly closed my eyes to rest.

    I had a lot of visitors come by, one of them being my father's brother and his wife. I found this kind of strange since I had never met either one of them before. He told me that he was the pastor of a Baptist church. They visited for a while and then asked if he could say a prayer for my recovery. After the prayer ended he said something that I didn't quite understand. He said I was a miracle.

    Over the next few days, I made incredible strides. The double vision I was suffering from was gone. The blurred vision had cleared up enough that I could now wear glasses. My appetite was coming back too. It took me a few days before I had a taste for food. The therapists were able to get me up and standing. I was regaining my strength. I was even able to hold onto both physical therapists like a crutch as they walked me up and down the hallway.

It had been several days since I had a shave and a shower. My wife requested a shave from the nurse. The nurse came into my room carrying a straight razor. "Mr. Cooper, don't move. I've never used this kind of razor before." I'm not sure if she was joking at this point, but she didn't have to worry about me moving my face. I stayed stiff as a board. I'd never had a shave from anyone using a straight razor before, and I valued my kisser more than that. I sat completely still until the shave was finished.

After a while, they prepared me for a shower. I leaned on the nurse as she guided me into the stall. She said I could hang my hospital gown on a rack by the wall and gave me shampoo and soap. "I'll be right outside if you need me for anything." I turned on the hot water and it felt so good on my face. I still had dirt on me from my accident. This was the first shower I had taken since the day of my accident. As I finished rinsing my hair, I turned to the side and slipped. I reached for anything I could get ahold of but came crashing down onto the soapy floor. I landed hard on my rump. With the medicine they had me on for pain, I didn't feel a thing. The nurse heard all the commotion and came running to my aid. She tried to help me, but she was so tiny and couldn't do much. I finally pulled myself up and she helped me get dressed. It really frightened the nurse when I fell. She had a panicked look on her face as she helped me back to the room. She explained the incident to my family and I never seen her again. They had a nurse supervisor come in and check me over. She said that was hospital protocol for insurance purposes. The only thing that was hurt was my pride.

    My wife went home to take a shower and get some clean clothes. My mother in law was there watching over me until my wife returned. This was my time to ask what happened to me. I knew my mother in law would tell me straight forward what happened. I turned to her and said, "Can I ask you something?" She said yes, what is it? "I want you to tell me the truth. What happened to me?" She explained to me that I got hurt working with my ATV out on the hillside. No one's really sure what happened. She wanted to know if I remembered anything about that day. I was kind of disappointed that I couldn't remember. In fact, I thought that I still lived in Columbus until she told me differently. I asked her if they had to put a steel plate in my head. She told me no, that the doctors used a compression tool to pull out the dents in my skull. I was satisfied with that answer, so I rolled over in the bed and slumbered back to sleep.

    My surgery went better than expected, and I was responding well to the recovery treatment. A nurse came in with what looked like a pair of pliers and a bowl. She smiled at me and said, "Today we will be removing your staples out of your skull." With a troubled look, I glared nervously at my wife for any kind of approval. She held my hand while the nurse began removing the staples. I heard a paw-ting sound when the nurse removed the first staple and it hit the stainless steel bowl. "Mr. Cooper only two hundred more staples to go." After a few more staples pulled from my skull, I asked if I could see my head. They found a mirror and I took a look. This was the first time that I got to see my head since the accident. I didn't think about it but the doctors had to shave my head for the surgery. I always had medium-cut black hair parted to the side. I'd never seen myself with a shaved head. All of my locks of hair were all gone. To make matters worse, my head looked like a baseball with stitching on both sides of my skull. I didn't mind looking the way I did, besides what could I do about it. Once I saw the new me, I knew I would never be the same again.

16

Broken

Have you ever watched a trainer break-in a horse? What a mysterious and exciting thing to witness. In training a horse you have to keep contact, meaning the horse must be engaged and stay focused on you as the leader. As long as the horse is engaged, the trainer rewards the horse's good behavior with breaks. The horse is allowed to stop and rest, while commanding and encouraging the next movement. The instructor pulls on the reigns as the horse gracefully maneuvers to the left or right. The instructor, with one swift motion, commands the horse to stop. The rider communicates to the horse a slow backup, proceed, and then gait.

This animal is being obedient to the instructor. Before the horse can be rode in this fashion, it must first be broken. A young horse can be strong willed and poorly disciplined. It takes patience and know how to prepare a young horse for riding. This is a process called saddle breaking. Once the horse is saddle broke, he becomes submissive to the rider and listens to his commands. Sometimes this is true for the believer too. Christians need to be "saddle broken" by God, before we can be useful workers for the Lord.

The dictionary best describes the word "broken" as an abrupt change in a person's character and attitude. When someone has been "broken" by God, He's brought their will in submission with His. We must first humble ourselves and submit to God's will before we can be true workers for the Lord.

Sometimes God has to prepare His followers to be able to serve Him. It all starts with the believer's attitude. Many people today let their attitudes stand in the way of submitting to the Lord. Arrogance, pride, and boisterous attitudes are just a few of the behaviors that can stand in the way of doing God's will. We must get our attitudes "in check," before we can fully serve Him. Stop and ask yourself this question: Are you more interested in yourself and what God can do for you, or what you can do for God? Once this pompous and proud person submits to God's will and is obedient, the Lord can use them for great and glorious things. Believers should always strive to be more like Christ in every way; even with our attitudes. In Philippians 2:5, Scripture instructs us to have an obedient attitude like Jesus. If we learn to be humble and obedient to God, He will guide us on the right path.

We can see many examples in Scripture of someone being "broken" by God, only to be used by Him later on to further the Kingdom of God.

The apostle Paul first comes to mind. Saul, who later was named Paul, was a murderer of Christians. When Jesus struck him down on Damascus road, Paul's will was shattered. Paul had a change of heart that day, but God knew Paul would not be usable as long as he was prideful and arrogant. God targeted his pride and arrogance, which would have prevented him from being a humble servant of God. To humble him, he was given a "thorn in the flesh." When Paul asked the Lord to remove this "thorn," The Lord told him that his grace is sufficient. Paul tells us this in 2 Corinthians 12:5-10: *For though I would desire to glory, I shall not be a fool; for I will say the truth: but now I forbear, lest any man should think of me above that which he seeth me to be, or that he heareth of me. And lest I should be exalted above measure through the abundance of the revelations, there was given to me a thorn in the flesh, the messenger of Satan to buffet me, lest I should be exalted above measure. For this thing I besought the Lord thrice, that it might depart from me. And he said unto me, My grace is sufficient for thee: for my strength is made perfect in weakness. Most gladly therefore will I rather glory in my infirmities, that the power of Christ may rest upon me. Therefore I take pleasure in infirmities, in reproaches, in necessities, in persecutions, in distresses for Christ's sake: for when I am weak, then am I strong.*

The disciple Peter had to be broken many times before he could serve the Lord faithfully. Peter was prideful and boastful before he was broken into submission by the Lord. One example is shown in Scripture when Jesus was explaining to His disciples that He soon would suffer and be crucified. Peter spoke up in a portentous way and made the statement that he wouldn't let that happen. Peter was going to do it his way and not the will of God. In Matthew 26:33 Peter says, *"even though all may fall away from you, I will never fall away."* Jesus told him that tonight you will deny Me three times before the rooster crows. Peter then proclaimed that even if I have to die, I will not deny you. Later that night a woman said that Peter was with Jesus, yet he denied ever knowing Him. Peter also denied Jesus twice more that very night. As Jesus walked by Peter he remembered what Christ had said and wept bitterly. He was completely broken down by the Lord. Peter repented and went on to be a great servant for the Lord.

For myself, I had to experience a fiery trial before I was submissive to God. I was living outside the will of God. I was more interested in what the Lord could do for me then what I could do for the Lord. I was too wrapped up in myself to put God first. I let everything in life come before God did. I was more interested in gaining material possessions than serving the Lord. I knew God should be first, yet I put Him last.

There is a price to be paid living outside of God's will. With God's chastisement, I was humbled and completely broken. My accident changed the very person that I used to be. God used my affliction to show me that not only life is precious, but I was in the wrong on so many things. He took away my pride and arrogance, and replaced it with the love of my Savior. Sometimes we must be completely broken before we realize God is calling us. Once we submit to God's will and become obedient to Him, we can be made whole again.

17

Time to Heal

*He lifted me out of the pit of despair,
out of the mud and the mire.
He set my feet on solid ground
and steadied me as I walked along.* **Psalms 40:2 (NLT)**

When I awoke from my coma, I was a different person. The Lord changed my heart. Looking around my room, everything had new meaning. I felt I now had a better understanding about life. This is hard to explain, but for the first time, life became real. I knew that only a miracle from God allowed me to survive a travesty of this magnitude. I had a lot of time to think about these things while lying in my hospital bed. Why did God pull me out of the fire? He must have a purpose for me, but what was it? I was forever changed by God's saving grace and wanted to do anything I could to repay Him. The Lord not only saved me physically but spiritually. Lying in bed, I realized that I had a second chance at life, and I was not going to waste it.

The day came when the doctors decided to take me off of a magical drug they called morphine. They were worried that if they didn't start weaning me off of it, I may soon become dependent. I was showing classic signs of dependency; I was now asking for it every half hour. The doctor's prescribed Lortab, to be taken every four hours. Lortab is a strong medicine that contains a combination of acetaminophen and hydrocodone. Hydrocodone is in the codeine family, which I am severely allergic too. This was clearly marked on all of my medical charts.

My wife went home to change clothes and rest. I remember my uncle and mother being the only family there at this time. The hospital was a little over crowded with new patients, so I was going to have to share a room. They started preparing another room for my new roommate and myself. The doctor prescribed Lortab and I instantly showed signs of an allergic reaction. My face and eyes started to swell. Between the Lortab poisoning and the lack of morphine, my mind went racing off to unfamiliar places. My whole body broke out in burning hives as I started to itch profusely. When my mother told the nurse that I was having a reaction, she said there was nothing that they could do until the medicine ran its course.

The nurse set me in the lounge while they prepared my new room. My mother went over to try and make sense of why they gave me a medicine that I was allergic too. I set there in pain and agony as my uncle began to talk with me. As I scratched both arms fervently, he told me that God could take away my pain if it was His will. He also told me that God could do anything. He then asked if I would pray with him. As we prayed together for God to take away my affliction, I could feel Jesus there in the room with us. I tried to look around while still in a haze from the bad medicine they gave me, but my eyes were almost swollen shut. We finished our prayer and I started to scratch. My uncle said, "Don't scratch. Trust in Him. He will give you the relief you are looking for."

I was delivered from my affliction by God. Shortly after our prayer, the pain, itching, and burning passed from my body. I started feeling better when I trusted in God to take away the pain. This might have been the first time that I actually called upon the Lord for help. He had been knocking at my heart's door for so long and I finally opened it. I realize now that I surrendered everything to my Savior right then and there. No more being stubborn. No more putting God last. Life became real. My life was finally full.

After about an hour, the hospital prepared my room. I cozied into bed and quickly drifted off to sleep. While sleeping, I had a dream that I'll never forget. This dream was set in the 1800's. It involved a man and a woman who were engaged to be married. The bride's family stood on one side of a plot of land and the groom's family on the other. The families had to layout and build a house together before they were to marry.

The bride went first and picked the layout she wanted for the kitchen. The groom picked next. He reviewed what the bride picked and then selected the layout for the sitting room. It was now the brides turn. She reviewed her first pick, his pick, and then decided on a bedroom over on the west wing. Every time someone would pick a room, my mind would fast forward through all the other options from the previous choices. The bride and groom made forty-six decisions before the house was agreed on. Each time a decision was made, my mind fast forwarded from the previous pick all the way through to the first pick. After my mind sped through the selections for the final time, they were pronounced man and wife.

    A few more days passed and I made tremendous steps in my recovery. It was going so well that it was now time to decide on an inpatient therapy center. This would be a place that would cater to my individual needs. It would allow me to heal at my own pace and provided the tools in order for me to do so. The closest center was in Columbus. I remember thinking, "I just came from there. Now they are trying to send me back." My wife had the hospital set it up. They told me that tonight would be the last night in this hospital.

    My last night at the hospital was miserable. It was around eleven at night, the hospital admitted another patient so we split the room. This man came in screaming in pain. The nurse that was assigned to us had prepped us for his arrival. She told us that he had been shot in the stomach twice in a robbery gone bad. He was a bystander, who had been shot in the crossfire. There was no sleep to be had. This man called out all night long. "Bring me something for this pain," he whooped and hollered every thirty minutes. I remember thinking, "Morning can't get here soon enough. It will be here soon and I can leave this place." I wanted to get on the road. I knew this hospital had done all they could do for me and it was time to move on. My goal was to get better, and I knew I had to go somewhere else to do it.

18

Thank God for Prayer and Family

Thank God for my family. They were there for me when I needed them most. My family was an integral part of my recovery process. They were praying and I was healing. Right from the beginning when the accident first happened, my mother and wife stopped to have prayer. They asked God to watch over and take care of me in this time of need. I wouldn't want to think about the outcome of this calamity without family and prayer.

I had many people to lean on during my recovery. I always had a friend or family member there visiting during the day. Seeing all the familiar faces was a great comfort to me. I grew to look forward to every visit, and was disappointed anytime I was alone. I would take family over any amount of gold. Family is the most precious treasure you can have in your life.

My wife is the strongest person I know. She got to witness God's miracle first hand. The doctors said the surgery was a success, yet they didn't give her much hope of a recovery. They just told her, "Let's wait and see." She had so much on her plate to deal with, yet she stayed strong during the entire incident. I remember when I first woke from the coma, they had an optometrist evaluate my eyesight. He told my wife that my peripheral vision was gone. This was the straw that broke the camel's back. She handled everything so well up until this point. I didn't understand why she broke down in tears at the time, but now I see. She could only handle so much worry, pain, and anxiety. I couldn't ask for a better wife. She's been there for me through thick and thin, for better or worse. She took care of me when I needed her most, and I am truly grateful that God sent me such a strong companion.

    My mother went out of her way to help me. She has always had my back in a time of need. She is a true friend. There are many things that she did to care for me in my time of need, I couldn't begin to write them down. I had the right two people with me during my accident that day. I counted on these two with my life. Thank God for my wife and mother.

    As with all my family, my aunt is a very special person. From a distance, she has always been there for me. She's like a super hero, working from the shadows and doing good deeds for those in need. I remember a time when I was eight, and she took me shopping. We went to the mall and I was allowed to pick out anything I wanted. I wasn't born with a silver spoon in my mouth, so this was a big deal to me. I picked out four or five outfits that lasted me all summer. It was always the little things like a shopping trip that meant a lot. She has been there for me and my cousins many times throughout the years.

    The day of my accident, she met my mother at the hospital. My aunt had worked at the hospital for over thirty years as a head nurse. She worked as a great interceder between my family and the doctors. She was able to explain to my wife exactly what was happening at all times. She was also a good shoulder to cry on. She was there for my family in so many ways that I cannot even begin to express. She was a valuable instrument in God's great plan.

    I could never say enough about the great blessings my mother and father n law have been to me. They took care of and consoled my wife when no one knew if I was going to live or die. I've always looked up to my mother and father in law. They have always been a great Christian influence on me. I know if I ever had a problem, I could go to them for counsel. They were both key instruments in prayer during my accident and recovery. I am forever grateful for having both of them in my life as mentors and friends.

    One of my uncles became a very special blessing to me while I recovered. He was there for me during this difficult situation. After working a full day, he came to the hospital most nights to check up on me. He too believed in Jesus as Lord, and was someone I could confide in. There were many occasions we had prayer together. He was there when I needed him the most and for that I will always be grateful.

My accident brought my family and friends together in prayer. Prayer was given on many occasions in the waiting room. Prayer chains from the local churches were created and put into action. My family also used social media tools like Facebook to reach friends from all over the country. With each prayer being answered, the chain grew stronger. People were praying across the Unites States, all the way from California to West Virginia. This was truly a trying circumstance for everyone involved; which brought my family closer together in this difficult time.

If it wasn't for the loving support of my family, I would not have recovered as fast as I did. They undoubtedly pulled together in my time of need. That's what a caring family will do. My family expressed their love and friendship when I needed them most. They gave me the strength and determination to heal. The Lord blessed me with a thankworthy family. One that I love dearly.

19

Back to Columbus? No Thank you

A new day was on the horizon. Today I would be transported to an inpatient rehabilitation hospital in Columbus. I just moved from Columbus a few weeks ago and I wasn't thrilled about returning. I was optimistic about getting better, and knew going back there was right. My wife decided this rehab facility would be better for my recovery. I made great strides in the last few days. It seemed like every day my body grew stronger and my thoughts became clearer. I heard the hospital I was going to was the best so I was eager to get there.

My father in-law pulled my wife's SUV to the front of the hospital loading zone, as a nurse wheeled me onto the pavement. The nurse pleasantly grinned and said, "Ok Mr. Cooper, you have a safe trip back to Columbus." I smiled and nodded ok as I stood up from the wheel chair. I pulled myself up into the SUV and shut the door. I made the comment to my wife a few weeks ago that I never wanted to go back to Columbus. It looks like now I will be there a long time.

While riding in the SUV, my eyes were playing tricks on me. Due to my recent injury, everything I saw in my rearview mirror was moving so fast that my eyes couldn't comprehend it. It all reminded me of a mosaic painting, with bright colors and shapes, and everything moved at the speed of light. The light outside looked broken and I saw lines moving in my vision. I spent most of the ride there with my eyes closed or looking down because it made me dizzy to stare straight ahead.

I didn't realize until we were almost there, that we were riding in my wife's SUV. I thought we were in my father in-law's vehicle the whole time. I couldn't understand why he had Elvis music in his vehicle. My wife and mother in-law made conversation in the back while I conversed about baseball with my father in-law. He was highly impressed that I remembered all the home run stats and batting averages of the all-time greats, especially after a major surgery.

When we arrived at the hospital, everyone greeted us with a warm friendly smile. One of the nurses showed me around the hospital while my wife finished up with registration. I was then asked to go to a room where they proceeded to ask me questions. Most of the questions were silly to me, and I found them entertaining. Questions like, "What is your name? Do you know what time it is? Is it daylight or dark out? Night or day?" I've been asked these questions many times before at the last hospital, so I answered them accordingly. I thought, "If someone didn't know the answers to these questions, they must be pretty bad off." I answered the last of the questions and the nurse said she would be right back. I asked her if this would be my new room. She told me no, that they have it scheduled for me to bunk with two other boys across the hallway. Well that was not going to work for me. I looked across the hall as the two boys yelled and screamed profanities at each other. I thought, "What kind of hospital is this?" I didn't realize that this hospital was equipped to handle mental patients.

My blood was beginning to boil so I asked her, "Where is my wife going to stay?" She sneered at me and said kind a snippy, "Not here." This didn't set well with me at all. Why didn't anyone tell me about this? They want me to stay in a room with two deranged out of their mind boys, and I can't even walk. What if I have to go to the bathroom? I barely had the strength to stand. There's no way that I could stay here with these two lunatics. I told the lady, "Well that's not going to work for me." The lady saw that I was getting agitated, so she told me that she would go get someone that could better assist me.

At this point I was ready to leave. They brought in another nurse who started off by asking those same interrogating questions. This time I wasn't as friendly. "Mr. Cooper is it daylight or dark out?" I didn't answer. She wrote something down and then said, "Can you tell me if it's morning or night?" I looked her square in the eye and said, "You tell me. Wait, if you are too stupid to know if its daylight or dark out, maybe you don't need to work here. Maybe I should be asking you the questions." That lady looked like she was about to cry as she stormed out of the room. I stood up and told my wife, "Let's go. I'm leaving. I'm not staying here one second longer. I held myself up against the wall and balanced myself enough to walk down the hallway. I made it to the lounge and found a place to sit. My mother and father in-law were in the lounge and asked me if everything was ok. I said, "It certainly is not. I'm not staying here with a bunch of idiots that don't even know if it's night or day out."

My wife filled them in on the details as I set angrily in a chair. About that time, here come two tough guys in white. I thought to myself, "I dare either one of them lay a finger on me. They thought they were going to bring some muscle in to push me around. That's not going to happen. I'm a Cooper, and Coopers were born to fight." Thoughts of my grandpa were running through my head. He was a scrapper and always told stories about how he didn't think twice about fighting those who done him wrong. I stood up and told the two guys in white, "You've got five minutes to find me a room or I'm going to whip everyone in the hospital." I turned to my father in-law and with a gruff look he said, "I wouldn't do that if I were you."

That got their attention as both men rushed off to go find a doctor. I was fuming mad and about to blow my top when two doctors walked up to me. The younger one said, "Mr. Cooper, I hear they aren't treating you fairly today. Here's what I'm going to do for you. I'm going to give you two options. I have it setup that you will have a room by yourself and your wife can stay there too and help you. Option two is I can discharge you right now and you can go home. As the doctor was telling me my options, I started to realize this guy looked just like a doctor on television. This guy looked like Doogie Howser. I started to chuckle a little while he finished talking. I told him, "All I ever wanted was a room by myself, and I need my wife to stay here and help me while I'm here. I didn't feel safe with those other two boys yelling and jumping up and down in the other room. I want to stay here and I want to get better. That's why I chose to come here in the first place." Doctor Doogie Howser smiled and said, "Fix up Mr. Cooper's room."

20

Clock. Cup. Rug.

Two mysterious men in white appeared. "It will take about thirty minutes to prepare your room Mr. Cooper." The nurse looked baffled at first. "They said his room was ready?" The men in white quickly replied, "The doctor ordered us to make some audio/video enhancements first. You want to watch some television while you're here don't you Mr. Cooper?" By this time I was extremely exhausted from the day's events, so I solemnly said, "Sure."

About an hour later, my room was ready to go. I laid down on the bed and quickly started to relax when another nurse walked in. "Is it okay if I ask you a few questions?" At this point I just wanted to nap. "It's okay, ask away." She lifted her clipboard and said, "Mr. Cooper, I would like to start out by asking you to remember these three words. Clock, cup." I already knew what was coming next, so I cut her off and said, "Rug." I was already familiar with these three words from the previous hospital. This was a memory exercise that we practiced every day. The nurse looked stumped. "How did you know that?" I wanted to make a joke and tell her that since my accident, I developed extrasensory perception. Due to my accident, I couldn't find the words to make the joke, so I simply explained to her that the previous hospital used the same memory exercise. I was still adjusting to my new found disabilities. My mind wouldn't allow my thoughts to work together. My head was still extremely swollen and my thoughts were foggy.

The nurse continued asking me other questions, which I breezed right through them. I thought those questions were too easy, so I started joking around with the nurse. She asked, "Mr. Cooper what would you do if you were at your house and it was on fire?" I looked at her and smiled, "Well first of all, I would call 911. Then I would probably go and hide." Well, let me tell you that is never the right answer to say when you are recovering from a head trauma. She was taken aback by my quick response. "Mr. Cooper if you went and hid till the firefighters arrived, you would die from the fire itself or smoke inhalation." I realized now that she took me seriously when I told my joke. It might've not been funny to her, but it was to me. I tried to explain to her I was just joking around as she started writing a book in my file. We eventually finished our interview and I immediately slumbered off to sleep.

It was now the beginning of the week and it was time to start my therapy classes. I was enrolled in three classes: Occupational therapy at nine in the morning, speech therapy at noon, and physical therapy at three. Occupational therapy was a class that prepared you to go back out into the workforce. We reviewed simple mathematics and problem solving equations. We even went on a field trip to Bob Evans. The goal was to order my food correctly, pay for it, and give the correct tip to the waiter. This was an important class, but it was the easiest for me. I was able to complete this class without any problems.

Speech therapy consisted of more clock, cup, and rug exercises. I filled out more worksheets in this class than the other two put together. This class was a lot like occupational therapy in the sense that we did a lot of problem solving. I remember one exercise in particular that was a bit confusing for me. I had to match up street addresses to the correct house on the worksheet. This was impossible for me at the time. Out of all the work that I did, this was the most confusing. The therapist said that this exercise would be the most challenging one for me because of the nature of my accident and where the damage was. She told me that once the swelling went down in my head, my thinking skills would come back and I would be able to better comprehend addresses.

Physical therapy was the most challenging class for me. I was now a former shell of who I used to be physically. I lost twenty-six pounds in two weeks, and most of it was muscle. I had a major problem with walking and running, my balance, and I lacked a lot of my former strength. I spent a lot of time in this class doing stretches and walking on a treadmill. I showed physical improvements every day. My balance was getting better and I was soon able to walk and stand by myself. This was a big step in my recovery. Although I still had moments that my body didn't want to cooperate, I was seeing quick results.

One of my assignments I had from my occupational therapy class was to shave, take a shower, and dress for the day without any help. This was the first time that I would attempt to do this completely by myself and I was a bit nervous. I started first with shaving. I still had no peripheral vision in my left eye, so this was going to be a challenge. The sides of my face were just a blur to me. I went over my face with the razor several times before I decided that was good. I ran my hand across my face and still felt stubble, but I figured it was good enough. I was nervous about taking a shower, since I fell in the shower less than a week ago. I placed my shampoo and soap where I could reach them. I held onto the safety railing to make sure my feet were firmly planted on the ground, before I turned on the water. The water started off ice cold, but I didn't want to move my feet; taking a chance of falling again. I would just have to suffer through it. Soon the water was warm enough and I finished my shower without another incident. I dried off before I got out of the shower. I figured with my luck, this would be for the best. I soon got dressed and was ready for my occupational therapy class. This was a major step in my road to recovery. I couldn't wait to get to class and tell the therapist the good news.

It had been a week since I started my inpatient therapy. The two men in white came back to my room with new instructions from the doctor. "Mr. Cooper, we will be turning off the video camera in your room while you go to your first class today." Video camera? Puzzled, I turned to my wife and asked her what they were talking about. She told me that they turned on a video camera, so they could watch me and make sure that I didn't have any anger issues or signs of being physically aggressive. At first I was a little upset when she told me that. "They don't know me. I would never hurt anybody." My wife turned to me and said, "Well less then 1 week ago, you threatened to fight everyone in the hospital unless you got a room by yourself." What could I say, she was right. "Well, I had a good reason a week ago." She followed up with, "You're right, they don't know you, that's why they turned on the video camera in your room." I cooled off real quick once I realized she was right. I was over the top that day, but I got my room.

Doctor Doogie came to my room as I was leaving for occupational therapy class to have a chat. "How are you feeling Mr. Cooper?" I answered, "I feel great. I'm getting stronger every day." He then said, "We have decided to give you an evaluation of your progress today. Your therapists will give you a final exam in each class and if you pass, you can go home. Do you have someone that could come get you?" My wife and I were very excited to say the least. We couldn't wait to get back home. It has been an emotional rollercoaster for both of us and we were ready for it to end. My wife told the doctor she would call her father to come pick us up.

My classes were assigned in a different order today with physical therapy first, speech class second, and occupational therapy last. I breezed right through my first two classes. I had a new swagger in my step today. Finally I was going home. Just one more class to go.

When I arrived to occupational therapy, I had to wait on the therapist to arrive. She showed up with what looked like two cake mix boxes. She explained to me that for my final exam, I would be baking either brownies or cookies, my pick. I thought, "What kind of final exam is this? The directions are right on the box." She said all I would have to do is to bake a yummy dessert, and I would pass the exam. "If you can make these cookies, I think they are going to let you go home today." You don't know how great that sounded to me.

I turned on the oven to 350 degrees and began mixing the batter together. After looking at both boxes, I decided to make cookies instead of brownies since there were less steps involved. I dipped out the cookie batter with a big spoon and placed the cookies in the oven, set the timer for twelve minutes, and then waited. With a ding from the timer signaling my cookie baking success, I picked up an oven mitt and laid those sweet savory cookies right on the stove top. "Mr. Cooper you did a fantastic job baking those cookies. There's one thing that you didn't do. Can you tell me what that step was?" I looked at her a little confused, but then it came to me. "Eat the cookies?" This wasn't the answer she was looking for. "No Mr. Cooper, you didn't turn off the oven." I didn't think about turning the oven off. I explained to her that I was too excited about going home today and that's why I didn't turn off the oven.

  The therapist excused herself from the class, but came back shortly with another instructor. "Mr. Cooper I am a counselor and a therapist. The board had their meeting and decided that you cannot go home today. You are still a risk to yourself. You didn't turn off the oven when you were done cooking. That could cause a fire and burn down your house." This news didn't not set well with my wife. She was visibly shaken. I guess it was from all the chaos that happened in the last few weeks. Her anxiety was building up like a pressure cooker and she was about to explode. She immediately said, "That's a simple mistake anyone could make. It would be different if it was his own house, and I don't think it's fair. The doctor said we could go home today. We've already called my dad to come get us. He drove over three hours and is probably out there right now waiting on us. This is crazy. Let me talk to your supervisor." I've never seen my wife this worked up before. I calmly turned to her and looked her in the eye. Her eyes told me the story. She was hurting inside. To ease her anguish a little, I spoke up and said, "Honey, I came here to get better. If the doctors think I need a few more days to get better then that's what I'm going to do. It's okay. Just call your dad and tell him it will be a few more days. I'm sure he will understand." She calmed down after I said this and agreed with me.

We made our way back to the room and my wife was still a little aggravated. She made a phone call to my father in law to see where he was at. She said, "Well you should just turn around now, they are not going to let us go home today. She started explaining to him my mistake in not turning off the oven. I knew I messed up and I was sorry. I felt very alone while she was talking on the phone.

Bright and early on the next morning, Doctor Doogie once again knocked on my room's door. "Mr. Cooper, how are you feeling today?" I told him that I was feeling much better after a good night's rest and I was excited to get the day started. He said, "Well I have great news. You have been released so you can go home today." My wife and I both looked confused, but we were excited about the good news. I said, "I don't understand. Why wasn't I allowed to go home yesterday?" He explained that the board met late last night and decided to release me. The real truth was this: I was being tested. The doctors were giving me one last test to see if I had any aggressive tendencies when I didn't get my way on something. They were playing mind games with me and my wife. I was being tested to see if I would explode like I did when I first arrived at the hospital. When they saw I wasn't a threat to anyone anymore, they released me.

I heard my wife make the phone call to my father in law. She said, "Can you come get us? They released him this morning. Yes I'm sure this time." Although we were very grateful this hospital was able to help me so quickly, we were both ready to go home.

Soon our ride arrived. We loaded all our belongings and were quickly on the road; headed for home. I was excited to make it back for one good reason. I couldn't remember the house I bought a few days before my accident. I also couldn't remember the house we just moved from. My memory was still cloudy. I thought of these things on the ride back. I couldn't remember the accident and my head was still very swollen. The doctors told me that my memory should come back after the swelling subsides. I still had a long road to travel, but I knew God was with me. I saw that He carried me through the accident and healed me in the matter of a few weeks. I knew He would allow me to get back to normal. I put all my faith in Him, and I trusted in Him to heal me.

21

Raw Snorgs

For the next month I had to go to an outpatient facility for therapy. My classes were scheduled twice a week, Tuesdays and Thursdays. Once again they were occupational health, speech, and physical therapy. My occupational therapy class mainly consisted of the therapist trying to distract me while I completed worksheets on math, spelling, and problem solving. She told me that in the work place I would be distracted, so I would have to focus on the work at hand and tune out all the outside distractions. She asked me what my profession was. When I told her that I sold cars, she told me that she didn't know how to prepare me for that kind of work. I explained to her that I used to be the sales manager and my accident didn't affect my selling abilities. I proceeded to tell her about the ten steps in purchasing a car. These steps would be what I would share with my new hires. We did a lot of math problems because my work did involve a lot of equations such as figuring payments with interest rates, and monthly terms. We worked on this for the rest of the month.

My physical therapy class was still the most challenging for me. I developed a nerve problem in my back, which felt like something cool was dripping down my back. I also had numbing sensations in my elbows and hands. We worked on different stretches and exercises to help with my new problems. We also focused a lot on my balance, which was still terrible. The therapist gave me an exercise chart to take home so I could do the exercises there too. He pinpointed the weaknesses that I developed after my accident, and focused on them. I was now able to walk and run freely, but standing on one leg without falling over was too much to handle for me. We spent most of the class time focusing on exercises that help with balance.

The most intriguing class by far was speech therapy. This class was nothing but mind games for me. I had the meanest therapist in town; until I figured out what she was trying to do to me. She tried to push my buttons on several occasions, but I wouldn't engage in her sarcasm and taunting. I remember coming out of class so worked up over her banter and ridicule that I felt like I was going to explode. Then it donned on me. That's exactly what she wants me to do. I figured out that she was pushing my buttons on purpose to see if I would yell back at her or show any aggressive reactions to her bantering. I guess she read my file from the other hospital. After I figured out what her game plan was, I ended up making her mad on several occasions, because I wouldn't partake in her rudeness. She soon figured out that I was on to her, so she ended that exercise. She turned out to be a really nice lady.

One day, I was having a rather difficult time with one set of worksheet exercises. The worksheet consisted of a bunch of sentences that ran together with other letters just thrown in the mix. The sentence read something like this: *Inthexsummer,omanyljpeopleliketoeatkfreshtvegetables.*
Theytarerusuallypreparedsrrawsnorgrilledxrt.

The sentences should have read: In the summertime, people like to eat fresh vegetables. They are usually prepared raw or grilled. The therapist only gave me three minutes to complete the exercise. I understood the first sentence and quickly wrote it down. I just couldn't comprehend the second sentence. I got, "They are usually prepared," right before the buzzer went off.

She asked me if I got it. I told her almost, but I couldn't finish the last sentence. She said, "Not a problem Mr. Cooper, let's walk through it together. Do you get any of the last sentence?" I had most of it figured out, but I couldn't get the ending. I said, "Here's what I got so far. They are usually prepared, I just can't get the rest." She said, "Ok Mr. Cooper, what does the next few words look like? Take a moment and think." I glared down at the sentence. "The next part looks like just gibberish to me. Does it really say anything?" She was now getting a little frustrated with me as she said, "Now Mr. Cooper, you know it does. Now look at it and tell me what it says." I studied it again. It still looked crazy to me. All I saw was rrawsnorgrilledxrt so I said, "I think that's a raw snorg." She started laughing hysterically. "Now Mr. Cooper, tell me exactly what a raw snorg is." I meditated on it only for a brief second, when it hit me.

  I knew exactly what a raw snorg was. I started to tell her but something made me stop. I'm glad I did. You see, when my cousins and I were all very young, we had wild imaginations. One day we invented mystical and magical creatures called toggles. These fuzzy and furry creatures were all very mean and lived in people's sock drawers. We had come up with many different variations of toggles such as: boggles, stroggles, froggles, oogle ogles, snarks, etc. At one time, we were so involved in toggles that we wrote toggle adventures. These stories involved such characters like: The toggle king Sebulbula Negassa. Trentor was his evil half-brother, who vowed to one day rule the world. All the toggles were bad except for one, which was Ralph the nice toggle. We even had a book that contained all the stories we wrote called the "Toggle Handbook of Knowledge and Wisdom." I knew without a doubt that a raw snorg was in fact a toggle. I also knew that if I told her what a toggle was, I would still be in therapy today. I refrained from telling her what I thought I knew.

    A few days after therapy, I asked my wife to take me to church. I was fixated on the idea of going and determined to do so. I had a lot of free time to think about life in general. I thought a lot about God and the fact that He protected me during my accident, so I wanted to go to His house. My wife and I also received several phone calls from a member of the little church on the hill, saying that he was thinking about us. In his voicemail, he usually asked how I was doing and hoped to see me at church soon. I had no idea who this gentleman was, and why he cared so much about me, so I also wanted to meet him.

    When I walked through the doors at church, everyone turned around and started shouting; overcome with joy. The preacher came over to the pew I was in and shook my hand. He said, "Here is the miracle we've been praying for." I also got to shake hands with the fella that called my house so many times. I was happy to see all these strangers expressing their love and happiness that I came to church. The preacher then said, "This man just survived brain surgery." What? They must have me confused with someone else. I'm sure they were mistaken, but after the service I asked my wife, "The preacher said that I had brain surgery. What was he talking about?" After many months, I was still clueless about what actually happened to me. My wife was hesitate to tell me at first, but went ahead. She told me the whole story.

I improved so much over the next month that the doctor decided to release me to go back to work. He wanted me to come into his office for a visit. I had my accident May 23rd. It was now August 10th. My head was still swollen and numb in places, but my thoughts were now clear and I had overcome most of my disabilities. "It's good to see you Mr. Cooper. You look great. Last time I saw you, it wasn't on the best of terms." This man helped save my life. I knew he was the tool God used in performing the surgery. I looked up to this man. We said some pleasantries while he studied the x-rays. He said, "I hope that next time you are on an ATV, you will wear a helmet." I was a bit nervous talking to him, since he did help save my life. I answered, "Nope." While I was gathering my thoughts, he cut in, "What do you mean? There were many people involved in your surgery. We all worked very hard for you. We didn't know if you were going to make it or not. The surgery lasted almost nine hours." I interrupted him this time. "I said, no because there wouldn't be a next time. I will never get on a four wheeler again." He started smiling, "I like that answer a lot better." I didn't mean to upset the doctor that helped save my life. I felt really bad. He went off on a tangent when I was gathering my thoughts together. After I told him I would never be on one again, he was relieved. "Mr. Cooper, I think you are ready to go back to work. Have my nurse write a work release for you." That was it. Time to see if I could make it now in the real world. This would be a major challenge, and I was ready to take the next step.

22

Today Is the Best Day of My Life

Years ago, a friend of mine gave me a badge that read, "Today, is the best day of my life." The badge was yellow in color with black writing. He wore one every day. One day I asked him, "Why do you wear that silly badge all the time?" He smiled at me and said, "Did the quote on the badge get you talking? It's a conversation starter." He had a valid point. He then gave me the badge off of his shirt. He said, "Here. Take this one. I order them by the hundreds."

I held onto this badge and didn't pay much attention to it until after my accident. I found it one day while ravaging through a box of miscellaneous junk. After everything I experienced over the last few months, I realized that every day I'm alive is the best day of my life. I proudly wore this badge on my first day back to work to remind me of this: Today, is the best day of my life.

The car business is usually cut throat. There's always sneaky underhanded salespeople that try and steal commissions and car deals from others. When I went back, I didn't expect it to be any different. The day I started work, everyone showed compassion towards me. I received hugs from all the office ladies, handshakes from the salespeople. My general sales manager even let me work every other day for the first few weeks until I got back in the groove of selling cars again. This was something he didn't have to do for me. The new car sales manager even told me that if I sell eight cars in the next two weeks, that he would pay me a bonus of five hundred dollars. I'd been out of car sales for a few months now, and he was worried that perhaps I wouldn't be as efficient as I once was. I told him not to worry about it; salesmanship is something I would never forget, "It's just like riding a bike." I knew I had to hit the bonus. I had a lot of bills to pay.

  I achieved my goal and sold eight cars in the last two weeks of the month, while working just every other day. I thought to myself, "I've still got it." As soon as that thought crossed my mind, so did another. "I." I didn't want to be an "I" guy anymore. I didn't want to be the guy that bragged about being the best and taking all the credit for everything. God gave me a second chance at life and this time I was going to do it His way. I knew that the only reason I sold eight cars in seven days was that God was still watching over me. He blessed me with the sales to help pay the bills. I'd been out of work for almost three months now and the bills were piling up. We still hadn't sold our house in Columbus. Thankfully I was able to sell my ATV on E-bay while I was out of work, to help pay some of the bills.

I didn't want to just pick up where I left off in life. I owed God more than that. I wanted to know more about the God that saved me. I once had the mentality to "believe and let it be." I was fine with that at one point in my life. I see now that I was foolish and naïve to believe that way. I didn't seek God until now.

I'd been going to church most Sundays now. I enjoyed listening to God's Word being preached on Sundays. One day I called the pastor of the little church on the hill, and asked him what I needed to do in order to be baptized. I figured that was a step I needed to take if I was going to truly be a servant of God. I felt that being baptized would take me to the next level in my life. I just wanted to be a servant of God in any way that I could, and I knew that being baptized was important.

The pastor told me that being baptized was just an outward confession that I am saved. He said I would be showing the world that I am a follower of Christ. That's exactly what I wanted to do. I believe with all my heart that Jesus is Lord and I wanted to share this with the world.

I will admit that I didn't know a lot about the Lord, but I was eager to learn. I saw things take place in my life over the last few months that couldn't have happened by accident. The doctors even told me that it was "Divine Intervention" that brought me through the surgery and recovery. I knew now that God had an even bigger plan for me.

It was time for me to sit everything else aside and put God first in my life. This is something that I'd never done before. I was always trying to do what others wanted me to do. I was also too busy trying to make a fortune to pay much attention to God. I knew that if I put Him first, everything else would eventually fall into place. I also thought that this might not be an easy accomplishment since I'd never tried to faithfully serve Him. I felt that God wanted me to, and that was good enough for me.

I held on to the thought that God spared me for a reason, but what was it? That reason was something that I now sought. I wanted to know what God had planned for me. I was a twenty-seven year old grown man, who hadn't matured spiritually. It was now time for me to put away all childish things. 1 Corinthians 13:11 describes just that: *When I was a child, I spake as a child, I understood as a child, I thought as a child: but when I became a man, I put away childish things.* That's what I now had to do.

23

One Last Ride

Are they not all ministering spirits, sent forth to minister for them who shall be heirs of salvation? **Hebrews 1:14**

We all have a time in our lives which we must decide to be faithful and serve God, or choose to be rebellious. I was now embarking on a new chapter in my life. I had a change of heart and a change of mind; my old ways were gone. I was now seeking God on a more personal and spiritual level. I was eager, hungry, and on fire for His Word, but I was very young spiritually. I had no idea that an attack from the devil was lurking upon the horizon. I didn't realize that on the day before my baptism, this soldier of God would be thrown right onto the front lines of the battlefield.

The dealership was having one of the biggest sales of the year. The manager hired ten outside salespeople to help with all of the extra traffic we were supposed to have. They mailed out over fifty thousand flyers to local area customers. The customer was guaranteed to win one of four prizes. You were guaranteed either a tool set, fishing pole, charcoal grille, or lottery scratch-offs just for coming by. They also had a special lockbox, that if your key opened it, you won a new car. As you could imagine, this brought everyone to the dealership. The problem with this sale was most people just wanted to see what they won.

 After talking to about twenty five people and not one of them were interested in buying a car, I was pretty discouraged. I thought, "This is a huge waste of time. No one wants to buy a car. They are just looking for something for free." While being depressed at this flop of a sale, I saw a customer heading over to the new cars with a sales flyer folded up and sticking out of his back pocket. I thought to myself, "Great another gift seeker." I made my way over to him. He threw up his hand and said, "Hey buddy. I don't want to buy anything, I just want to see what I won." I introduced myself and welcomed him to our dealership. "Come on inside and we will get you registered." We set down, and I began to fill out the registration. "What is your name?" He quickly stopped me and said, "This might save some time sir, here's my card." I examined his business card intently, and saw that he was a pastor. "So you're a pastor?" He proudly said, "Yes I am. I've been a pastor for over thirty years now." I had a new interest in my customer. With a refreshed spirit, I thought maybe he could answer a question or two. I began by telling him about the accident I had, and how God brought me through it. I explained to him I wanted to repay God for giving me a second chance at life. I asked him, "What do I need to do to be closer to God? How can I serve Him?"

This bit of information caught the pastor by surprise. I guess he thought all car salesmen were crooks, and maybe most are, but not this one. He too had a new interest in the conversation. My new friend proceeded to tell me that he started to put the sales flyer in the trash but something convinced him not to. He said he saw now that it was God that brought him to the dealership today to talk with me. When he told me that I looked at him intrigued, as more questions popped into my head. He continued to say, "To answer your question, you need to be saved." I told him that I was saved at the age of fourteen. He then asked me, "Have you been baptized yet?" I told him that I was actually scheduled to be baptized tomorrow. He explained to me that being baptized is an outward confession to show the world that I believed in Jesus Christ as Lord and Savior. I told him that I believed in Jesus and wanted to be closer to Him, but I didn't know how. He told me the best way is to read the Bible. He exclaimed, "All the answers you seek are there in the Good Book. Once you read it, God will reveal to you all the answers you are seeking. Trust in the Lord and He will guide you along life's journey." He then asked if we could have prayer. We were sitting in the middle of the showroom with about fifty people next to us but I didn't care. I knew that this man was sent by God.

He asked if we could to pray to God that I would stay strong for my baptism. I didn't understand this request at the time. I told him yes. We bowed our heads together. We prayed to God about my upcoming baptism and that I would go on to be a great disciple for the Lord. I realized we just had church right there in the middle of the showroom. After the prayer ended, I thanked him and got him his gift. He didn't win the car, but that was to be expected. We knew God brought us both together for a reason.

It was soon time to leave work, so I got in my car and headed down the interstate. I turned the radio down low so I could think about what the pastor shared with me earlier in the day. I meant the things that I told him. I wanted to know God like never before. I didn't know a whole lot, but I knew He saved me and blessed me with a second chance to do things right. I wanted to serve Him.

While driving down the road, I started to think about tomorrow's baptism and how it would all play out. Most of my family would be there watching me. After the baptism, we all planned to meet at my house for a picnic. While I was thinking about all of this, a nervous and uneasy feeling came over me. I started to feel sick at my stomach as my mind raced with apprehension. "I can't do this. I'm not ready. I can't get baptized." My hands started to shake while firmly gripping the steering wheel. "I can't get up in front of all those people tomorrow. There's no way." I broke into a cold sweat and felt like I was going to pass out. "What is happening to me?" Everything was telling me no, not to go through with it. I struggled with this feeling for several minutes. I thought, "Is this from God? Why would God try and talk me out of being baptized?" after a moment, I knew this feeling of sickness and doubt was not from God. This was an attack from the devil.

    I didn't even see it coming. I was blindsided from the enemy while driving home from work. The devil knew my plans were to seek God and draw closer to Him. I see now what the pastor was talking about when he asked if we could pray that God would keep me strong for my upcoming baptism. Somehow he knew I would later struggle with this. Was the pastor part of God's plan for me? Was he one of God's messengers sent to give me strength? Perhaps. I think the pastor was used by God as a weapon and a blessing. I didn't know at the time that I would later be tempted by the devil. The devil threw everything he had at me to convince me not to go through with the baptism and to follow God, but the Lord kept me strong. Here's what the devil didn't realize. I was already one of God's children and there was nothing that the devil could do to stop me from being baptized.

    I remember this next part very distinctly. I had fear and doubt covering every inch of my body. My hands trembled as my eyes started to tear up. Suddenly, something took hold of me, and a huge smile came over my face. I was grinning from ear to ear, as my heart was overflowing with God's love. In a split second all my worries and fears subsided and turned to happiness and contentment. I said in a loud convinced voice, "I wouldn't miss my baptism for the world." I knew then and there, it was the devil trying one last time to get me to change my mind. He tried his hardest that day to convince me that I didn't need God and too forget about Him. God, who is in control, had other plans.

There comes a time when we must choose our sides. In Luke 11:23, Jesus says you are either with me or you are against me. I stand with Jesus Christ. Which side are you on?

24

War of the Worlds

For we wrestle not against flesh and blood, but against principalities, against powers, against the rulers of the darkness of this world, against spiritual wickedness in high places.
Ephesians 6:12

Have you ever been sitting at the office on a slow, uneventful work day? This can be very stressful, as it feels like time stands still. As the day lingers on, not a fax, tweet, or even an email to digest. As the phones remain quiet, you wonder where all the customers have disappeared to? Turning to your associate to discuss the day's lack of business, the conversation quickly evolves into the Gospel of Jesus Christ. Maybe God has put something on your heart that you need to share with your co-worker, or perhaps your cohort is unsaved and God is dealing with this person. Whatever the reason, it seems like when the meat of the conversation comes to fruition, this always happens: A page over the intercom, asking one of you to leave the office. At the most inopportune time, the phone rings profusely, prohibiting you from answering any questions they might have about our Savior Jesus. Whatever the situation is my friend, you get the point. There are spiritual powers at work in this world today, which will do anything necessary to prohibit Christians from sharing the Gospel to those who seek it, and those who need to hear it for the first time.

Living a Christian life is not a playground. It is better described as a tumultuous battleground. Christians are continuously fighting a spiritual war against evil. The battle between these two kingdoms has existed since the beginning of time. We have evidence from Genesis to Revelation. Once you accept Jesus Christ as Lord and Savior, you are immediately brought into war against the adversary; who would like nothing more than to see you fail in your relationship with God Almighty. Evil is all around us, and it's now time for Christians to wake up, suit up, and engage.

We need to realize that every Christian is an integral part to God's plan. We must equip ourselves with God's Word, not only to keep us focused and strong, but also as a tool to reach the unsaved. Jesus instructs us to do this in Mark 16:15. We need to reach out and share the Gospel to the world. Our hope for the unsaved is that they may come to know Jesus as Savior before it's too late. The battle lines have been drawn, and it's up to us to further God's work. Christians need to understand that we are in a war against an enemy that will stop at nothing to slander and defame our Christian values.

Did you know that you are hated? If you are a believer in Christ, the devil and his army want to destroy everything about you. This hatred for Christians positions us constantly in the enemy's sites. The devil cunningly attacks Christians with his "wiles." The definition for the word "wiles" refers to someone being tricked into deceit or craftiness in a planned way. It is considered a well-planned out deceit. The devil is known to attack when you least expect it, especially when you are weak. Jesus warns us to be alert and pray; to keep vigilant so we will not be deceived. Matthew 26:41 says: *Watch and pray, that ye enter not into temptation: the spirit indeed is willing, but the flesh is weak.* The devil thrives on your weakest idiosyncrasies, characteristics, and habits. The great deceiver attacks Christians through the fleshly desires of the world. John 2:16 tells us: *For all that is in the world, the lust of the flesh, and the lust of the eyes, and the pride of life, is not of the Father, but is of the world.* The devil is cunning and knows exactly what sin to tempt you with.

    So what is our weapon we should use against the wiles of the devil? We must use God's Word through prayer to ward off the temptations we face from our attacker. 2 Corinthians 10:4 says: *For the weapons of our warfare are not carnal, but mighty through God to the pulling down of strong holds.* The Gospel of Matthew talks about Jesus being tempted by Satan in the wilderness. Jesus resisted the devil's temptations by quoting the Word of God. Jesus resisted the devil and he fled. We must keep strong and loyal to God anytime an attack occurs. Only then will we defeat the adversary.

In Ephesians 6:11, Paul instructs the believer to put on the full armor of God, to combat and withstand the wiles of the devil. Paul explains how to defeat the wiles of the devil in Ephesians 6:12-18 NLT: *For we are not fighting against flesh-and-blood enemies, but against evil rulers and authorities of the unseen world, against mighty powers in this dark world, and against evil spirits in the heavenly places. Therefore, put on every piece of God's armor so you will be able to resist the enemy in the time of evil. Then after the battle you will still be standing firm. Stand your ground, putting on the belt of truth and the body armor of God's righteousness. For shoes, put on the peace that comes from the Good News so that you will be fully prepared. In addition to all of these, hold up the shield of faith to stop the fiery arrows of the devil. Put on salvation as your helmet, and take the sword of the Spirit, which is the word of God. Pray in the Spirit at all times and on every occasion. Stay alert and be persistent in your prayers for all believers everywhere.* In 1 Peter 5:8, Peter describes the devil as a roaring lion, looking for prey to consume. It reads: *Be sober, be vigilant; because your adversary the devil, as a roaring lion, walketh about, seeking whom he may devour.* The devil wants to seek and destroy the truth that is Christianity. We must be vigilant against the wiles of the devil by holding onto our faith in God.

The devil creates lies about who God is, God's plan of salvation, and the desires God has for our Christian lives. He uses lies from unbelievers as a primary weapon. John 8:44 describes the devil as a murderer and the father of all liars, and there is no truth in him. It reads: *Ye are of your father the devil, and the lusts of your father ye will do. He was a murderer from the beginning, and abode not in the truth, because there is no truth in him. When he speaketh a lie, he speaketh of his own: for he is a liar, and the father of it.*

This cunning deceiver's goal is to destroy everyone God has put on this earth. The devil's objective is for the unbeliever to keep on unbelieving. The devil wants nothing more than the unbeliever to reject Jesus Christ and spend all of eternity in Hell.

The devil has blinded the eyes of the unbeliever with his worldly craftiness. The Bible states in 2nd Corinthians 4:4 NLT: *Satan, who is the god of this world, has blinded the minds of those who don't believe. They are unable to see the glorious light of the Good News. They don't understand this message about the glory of Christ, who is the exact likeness of God.* If your mind is blinded to spiritual things, then you won't be able to understand spiritual things. This clever deceit is of the devil. It is up to the believer in Christ to proclaim the Gospel to the world, in hopes that the unbeliever will repent and accept Jesus Christ as Savior, before it's too late. Today is the day of salvation, and it's up to every man to accept it. The gift of salvation is never forced upon you. You have the option to accept it or reject it. The choice is yours.

To better understand what this war entails, we must first touch upon the history of the battle, our allies, and the attacker. First and foremost the Holy Trinity: God the Father, God the Son, and God the Holy Spirit. These three spirits represent the Holy Trinity and are one in the same. God is the Supreme Creator of the Heavens and earth, and everything in them. He is perfect, Holy, and righteous.

Our Lord is all powerful. He is omnipotent, omnipresent, and omniscient. The Greek word "omnipotent" translated here is *pantokrator*, meaning "Almighty." He has full authority and reigns over all creation. The Bible is robust in declaring this truth. Revelation 19:6 reads: *And I heard as it were the voice of a great multitude, and as the voice of many waters, and as the voice of mighty thunderings, saying, Alleluia: for the Lord God omnipotent reigneth.*

The Lord God is omnipresent. The term *omnipresent* means to be present everywhere at the same time. God is observing all that is good and evil in the world. In Numbers 32:23, the Bible tells us that your sin will find you out. God knows and sees all: past, present, and future.

God is also omniscient. The Merriam-Webster online dictionary defines omniscient as one having infinite awareness, understanding, and insight. We serve a great and glorious God who has the power and authority to do anything. God is absolute, unlimited, supreme, everywhere, and all knowing. God is Spirit, and because of that, He is capable of being omnipotent, omnipresent, and omniscient.

Angels are servants of God that assist Him in carrying out His plans and purposes. The word "<u>Angel</u>" actually comes from the <u>Greek</u> word *aggelos*, which means "messenger." Hebrews 1:14 tells us that angels are ministering spirits sent by God to encourage the "heirs of salvation." Many of us have unknowingly been visited by, or come into contact with angels. Hebrews 13:2 says: *Be not forgetful to entertain strangers: for thereby some have entertained angels unawares.*

When God created the angels, he also created an angel named Lucifer: aka the devil, aka Satan. The name "Satan" comes from a Hebrew word meaning an adversary, the enemy, and the accuser. Call him what you will, but this great deceiver resents God and stands for everything that our glorious God is not. The devil would like nothing better than to sever or interrupt your Christian walk with God, in any way he can.

Contrary to what most people believe, Satan was not always an evil supernatural being. He was an angel created by God; full of beauty and power. He was the chief musician in Heaven before he tried to overthrow God. That's why some of today's music is heavily influenced by evil. The Bible calls him the angel of light and the prince of this world. Today, the devil influences all the evil that is done.

The devil is encompassed with the sins of pride and covetousness. Lucifer, better known as "Satan," along with a third of the angels, rebelled against God in Heaven. He wanted to overthrow God, and lusted to be the supreme ruler over everyone. He wanted to reign over both the Heavens and earth. There was a great war in Heaven, and the devil and his demons were cast onto this earth. We read about the battle here in Revelation 12:7-9: *And there was war in heaven: Michael and his angels fought against the dragon; and the dragon fought and his angels, And prevailed not; neither was their place found any more in heaven. And the great dragon was cast out, that old serpent, called the Devil, and Satan, which deceiveth the whole world: he was cast out into the earth, and his angels were cast out with him.* Since the battle in Heaven, the devil and his minions have tried to destroy everything that is of God here on earth. He deceived Adam and Eve in the Garden of Eden, and has betrayed and conned man ever since.

The world is changing. It seems like the spirit of the antichrist is all around us. When I say the spirit of the antichrist, I mean things that are not of our Lord Jesus Christ. Just because the antichrist hasn't risen to power yet, doesn't mean he's not at work. It seems like there are a few government officials in this world who are under the influence of the antichrist. These select few have power, wealth, money, and the ability to change laws to better suit their cause. They have taken Christ out of our school system. They teach about Buddha, Mohammad, and others, but Christ is not allowed? It just doesn't make much sense. You can't even have prayer at a high school football game in the name of Christ.

The devil is heavily influencing our music, television shows, movies, and anything else he can weasel his way in to. He has taken control of the internet, and polluted our minds with internet porn and deceptions. The devil is trying to do everything he can to pollute God's work. The spirit of the antichrist is even creeping into some of our churches.

Just a few months ago a Methodist church pastor, only a few miles down the road from my church, gave a startling announcement to his members the other day. After visiting the Methodist convention, the new pastor or bishop stood in front of the church and proclaimed, "Today is a new day." He announced to the members that they will no longer be taking a stand against abortion or homosexuality. He stated that taking a stand against these things isn't politically correct, and they will no longer support being against them at this church. He said it was a new day and that was the old way of thinking. He also stated that some curse words would slip out of his mouth from time to time while at the altar, but not to worry, "It's a new day."

This "new day" way of thinking is of the spirit of the antichrist. It is against God and the Bible. The Lord had the Bible penned by the prophets, so that we know and understand His Word and Commandments. Man cannot change God's Word to be politically correct. The Lord tells us to fear Him and keep His Commandments. People that do not take the Lord's word seriously are headed for absolute failure. 1 Corinthians 1:18 NLT says: *The message of the cross is foolish to those who are headed for destruction! But we who are being saved know it is the very power of God.*

Call to action:

We need to get off the pews and get into battle. We as Christians need to band together against the enemy. Christians need to get involved and take back our school system, laws, and our country before it's too late. It does matter who you vote for at election time. We need to remember elections have consequences.

The enemy is trying earnestly and whole heartedly to wreck our fellowship and personal walk with God. John 10:10 reads: *The thief cometh not, but for to steal, and to kill, and to destroy: I am come that they might have life, and that they might have it more abundantly.* We must educate ourselves on how to defeat Satan and his army; which means we must read the Bible. Reading God's Word will supply us with the proper tools to defeat our foe.

We need to realize that we are in a spiritual battle against Satan and his demons. We cannot give in to the devil with our worldly desires. Ephesians 6:11 states that we need to stand firm against the enemy; especially when a temptation arises. Christians will have victory over Satan when we plant our feet and stand in the truth; knowing that Jesus Christ is right there with you.

Spoiler Alert:

Be of good cheer my friend. If you turn to the end of the Book of Revelation, you will see that we win in the end. The devil knows he only has but a short time. This is why he is trying in every way to create chaos on earth. The devil, his demons, and all the unbelievers, will one day be cast into the lake of fire; and that's where they will be imprisoned for eternity.

Stay steadfast:

Just because we know we win, doesn't mean we can sit around and do nothing. Jesus gives us instruction to get the Gospel out to the world. We must tell everyone we come in contact with, who hasn't heard the Gospel, about our Lord Jesus Christ and His plan of salvation. We as Christians need to ban together. Stay strong friend, by reading God's Word daily. Keep loyal and true to Him. We need our Christian battle cry to echo throughout our land and the world.

25

A Lesson from Hesson

Then he said to the crowd, "If any of you wants to be my follower, you must turn from your selfish ways, take up your cross daily, and follow me. **Luke 9:23 (NLT)**

I will admit that I stumbled a bit out of the gate. I was recently baptized and wanted to serve the Lord in any way I could. The problem was that I didn't realize that my attitude was not quite in check yet. Even though I was humbled by my accident, I still had some of the "old" mind set and mentality still lingering. I was now playing for the winning team and didn't care who might be offended when I spoke the truth. I was still a bit stubborn and cocky. I needed to grow.

I just started reading the Bible on my lunch break. My knowledge of the Bible was still very limited. I had an hour for lunch, so on my break I would eat and then read. Due to my accident, I could only read the Gospel for about twenty minutes each day before my eyes would start to cross, blur, and hurt. I was faithful in my studies, and would read every day that I worked. Since I failed reading the Bible in the past, this time I started reading the New Testament first. I knew that's where I would find Jesus. I wanted to know Him and I wanted to know the truth.

The more I read the Bible, the wiser it made me. I came across something while reading one day that I took to heart. In the Bible I read that I shouldn't have a know-it-all attitude, and that I should humble myself and submit to the Lord. I read that God hates a prideful heart. I was very prideful and proud of my accomplishments. This was something that I knew I would struggle with going forward.

After reading one day, I began to meditate on His Word. "What does being prideful really mean?" I thought about it some more. I came to the conclusion that being prideful is about me and only me. Let me explain. I worked hard to provide for my family. I did everything that I could for my family. I thought some more and then realized that my heart was in the right place, but I left God out of the picture. I wouldn't have been able to provide for my family without God blessing me. It was God who provided me with a good job and blessed me with all my accomplishments in life. It was God who gave me houses, cars, and everything else I've ever dreamed of. It was all God. I didn't do anything. I got down on my knees and asked God to forgive a fool like me and I thanked Him for showing me the truth.

Believe it or not, I haven't worked with many Christians in the car business. When I came back from Columbus everything at the dealership had changed. I was the boss when I left, now the new boss was a self-professed atheist. He bragged to everyone that would listen about how he thought there is no God. He told everyone that he was an evolutionist. He said there is no Heaven or Hell, so live it up while you can. What a sad way to believe.

The good news was there were a few Christians working there too. I could tell who the Christians were right away, just by watching them. They didn't act like the new boss and his buddies. You could tell just by their actions they were believers. I didn't know that I would soon be classified as "one of them" by the new boss. Our dealership was divided. I was labeled an outcast by all of my former friends so I became a loner of sorts. Every now and then, one of my Christian buddies would talk to me, but they were loners too.

I worked with a friend that I trusted and relied on to help me with my Christian walk. We all had nicknames at work. If you fit into the "in" crowd, you got a nickname like "Rattlesnake" or "Bucket Head." The rest of us were called by our last names. I was Cooper and he was Hesson. We knew what they were doing and thought it was quite funny to label us that way. I looked up to Hesson. He grew up in a Christian church, married a Christian girl, and professed to everyone that he was a Christian. He never smoked, drank, or did drugs; something we both had in common. I admired the fact that he didn't take no lip from the unsaved about his faith.

I enjoyed our conversations together. Usually after lunch, I would come back with something I found fascinating that I just read from the Bible. I couldn't wait to talk to him about it. One day the conversation led to the discussion of which version of the Bible is correct. I asked, "So which version of the Bible do you read?" He said, "I read from the New Living Translation." I couldn't believe my ears. "What?" What's wrong with the King James Version?" He grinned and said, "You sound just like my dad. That's all he will read from too. I read from the New Living Translation and the American Standard Version because they are easier to understand." I remembered the church that I went to in Columbus, where the Bible they were reading from added words to the story that my Bible didn't have. I just read in the Book of Revelation, where it distinctly says not to add or take away from the Bible, or your name will be blotted out of the Book of Life. It also said you will receive all the plagues that are written in the Bible. I told Hesson this and he replied, "The King James Bible is just a version too. Does that make it wrong?" Hesson had a good point.

The conversation had become rather loud and started drawing attention. We both felt we were in the right. Hesson did the right thing and walked away. I wasn't done and so I followed after him. We made it to the parts counter and I grabbed his arm. "Let me ask you this? Aren't you afraid that you are reading the wrong book?" I see now that I was clearly in the wrong, and I didn't understand the verses of Revelation correctly. This can happen to someone that is new at reading the Bible and doesn't have a lot of knowledge under their belt. It says in the Book of Revelation, that you are not to add or take away from the Bible, I just missed the meaning. The verse wasn't referring to the different translations of the Bible.

At this point, we were drawing a crowd again, as our conversation turned into an argument. Hesson looked around and saw the unsaved all around us, listening to the argument. He looked at me and said, "C'mon. I need to talk to you." I followed Hesson into the garage. He said, "Let me ask you this." I could tell by his expression on his face that he was serious. "What are we arguing about exactly?" I started to reply and he cut me off." I'll never forget this next part. He brought me down from my high and mighty pedestal with these next words. He said, "Listen to me. What does it matter if Jesus picked up a rock and skipped it to the other side of the river? If the structure of the Gospel stayed the same, then what does it matter? If the meaning of the story is the same, then it shouldn't matter if he picked up one rock or three? What if at the end of the day someone gets saved when reading a different translation other than the King James? Sometimes it's just easier to understand. Let's face it, you had us arguing about the Bible in front of a crowd of the unsaved. I'm sure they are talking about us right now."

Wow. He was exactly right. I humbled myself and accepted my defeat. I apologized to Hesson and told him that I didn't see it that way. I told him that I didn't realize that our argument created a crowd. He said, "I know that you are on fire for the Lord. I can see that and I am so proud of you. You are doing great things, but make sure you have all the facts before you attack someone for their beliefs. We are on the same side. We need to act like it." I didn't realize that's what I was doing. I just thought it was a conversation that got way out of control. He was in the right, so I humbly apologized again.

NLT 2 Timothy 2:23-25 explains: *Again I say, don't get involved in foolish, ignorant arguments that only start fights. A servant of the Lord must not quarrel but must be kind to everyone, be able to teach, and be patient with difficult people. Gently instruct those who oppose the truth. Perhaps God will change those people's hearts, and they will learn the truth.*

I learned a lot from Hesson's lesson. He showed me there was a time and place for hot discussions about the Bible, and not to involve the unsaved when it came to who is right and who is wrong. He was also completely right about the different versions of the Bible. As long as the story and meaning stays the same, how you arrived there doesn't matter. I was young at heart in my dedicated Christian walk, and I didn't realize that I could have caused more harm than good, arguing in front of the unsaved. Christians need to be careful that they do not fall into the same trap as I did. I am now very careful in expressing my thoughts, especially around the unsaved. Hesson, lesson learned.

26

Soldier of Misfortune

If we are unfaithful, he remains faithful, for he cannot deny who he is. **2 Timothy 2:13 NLT**

Do you understand why Jesus died on the cross for you and me? God's plan of salvation is simple, yet some people do not fully comprehend it. His plan of redemption might best be easily summed up like this: We all have sin in our lives, and God demanded a payment for these sins. Since life is in the blood, God required a blood sacrifice as remittance. The Lord sent His Son Jesus Christ into the world to pay our sin debt. Jesus loves us so much that He freely died for our transgressions; to save all who believe in Him from a burning eternal Hell. *But he was wounded for our transgressions, he was bruised for our iniquities: the chastisement of our peace was upon him; and with his stripes we are healed.* Isaiah 53:5. A great man once told me that Jesus Christ wrote a check for the payment of our sins when He died on the cross of Calvary. In the memo He wrote, "Payment for all sin." Three days later the check cleared when He defeated death and rose again. Our Savior is alive today.

Everyone's probably familiar with John 3:16: *For God so loved the world, that he gave his only begotten Son, that whosoever believeth in him should not perish, but have everlasting life.* Jesus knew no sin; yet He made payment for our sins in full when He died on the cross. He paid a debt He didn't owe because we owed a debt that we couldn't pay. God accepted His Son's death as substitution for our transgressions. In Isaiah 53:10 the Bible tells us that it pleased the Father to bruise Him; to make His soul an offering for our sins. God loved us so much that He gave the world a gift in His Son Jesus; to die on the cross for everyone's sins. The rest is now up to us. All we have to do is believe in Him, and we too will have everlasting life.

The basis for all forgiveness is the atoning death of Jesus Christ. Leviticus 17:11 says: *for it is the blood that maketh an atonement for the soul.* Christ's death is the ultimate sacrifice to God for our sins. He died for the sins of the world. Jesus bore everyone's sins at the day of Calvary. This was all part of God's glorious plan of salvation. 1 Peter 2:24 explains: *Who his own self bare our sins in his own body on the tree, that we, being dead to sins, should live unto righteousness: by whose stripes ye were healed.* Christ's atoning death allows us to one day enter God's beautiful kingdom and spend eternity with Him.

Some people cannot fathom the simple plan of salvation God has laid out before us. They get too caught up in their past sins and never repent, or they think that their sin is too great for God to forgive. The Bible tells us there is only one sin that God will never forgive, and that's blasphemy of the Holy Spirit. God will not forgive the person that blatantly rejects the Holy Trinity. This isn't talking about the foolish person who said they don't believe there is a God and later realizes they were wrong. The unforgivable sin is the total rejection of God till the day that person dies.

God wants to forgive the sinner no matter how great the sin is. John 1:9 reads: *If we confess our sins, he is faithful and just to forgive us our sins, and to cleanse us from all unrighteousness.* Once you confess and repent of your sins, God will never bring them up again, especially to use against you in any way. God forgives you and forgets the sin. Psalms 103:12 shows us this: *As far as the east is from the west, so far hath he removed our transgressions from us.* God will never persecute you of your past sins once you've repented. If those thoughts enter your mind, they are of the devil.

I once worked with a man while selling cars, who was a retired Marine. He was the epitome of what everyone called a jarhead. He was tall in stature, a muscular build, and sported a nicely trimmed crew cut with both sides shaved to the skin. He came off as arrogant and cocky. He often said that he served his time in the Marines for our country and it was now time that the America repaid him for everything that he had to go through. I didn't pay much attention to that. I actually tried to keep my distance from him, because of his imperious and distasteful ways.

    This man often bragged that he knew everyone in Lincoln County. He would overhear a customer talking about it during a deal and would walk up to them and ask if they knew so and so. They would eventually find someone they both knew. He would then tell the customer, "I thought I knew you from somewhere." We nick named him "Lincoln County" because he claimed to know everyone that lived there.

    He soon noticed that I was not like all the rest and started to treat me differently. This man respected the fact that I was a Christian. After a while, we grew to tolerate each other in our own ways. You could tell from his stories and rants that he was not a Christian. He was always rambling on about how he found ways to cheat on his wife, how he got mad drunk at a party, and other nauseous obsessions.

    One day I was standing in the service bay, enjoying a water. This was a particularly hot and humid day, so I was trying to stay hydrated best I could. It was also a rather slow work day. During a slow work day, the salespeople tended to gossip with one another to make time go by. Looking through the glass door, I saw Lincoln County headed my way. He made his way under the garage door and said, "I've been meaning to talk to you about something." I first thought, "Oh boy. Here comes a bunch of nonsense." He sat down in one of the service chairs by the service counter and in a whisper said, "I know you're a Christian, so I have some questions for you." Lincoln County had my attention. "What can I help you with?" He lightly said to me, "I've been a horrible person. Why should I care about anything? God will never forgive me and I know I'll go to Hell for the things that I've done." I was taken aback at first. That was a lot to swallow. I said, "God is able to forgive all sin, no matter how great or small." His complexion turned pale white. "He can't forgive the things that I've done." He proceeded to tell this story: "There's a lot that you don't know about me. I served two terms in the Gulf War. I saw a lot, and I've done a lot of evil. My platoon once had orders to kill and destroy everything in a targeted small town. Men, women, and children; we basically killed anything that moved. Intelligence told us that this small town was harboring known terrorists. I had to do it. I had my orders." I interrupted him, "Look man, if your orders were to do that then you had no choice. You were fighting a war." He continued. "Have you ever heard about the spoils or war?" He started speaking very softly to me. "We hated the enemy with a passion, so we did some bad things. I remember when my infantry first marched into the small Iraqi town. The people were chanting for us. They thought we were there to help." His tone suddenly changed to sorrow and regret. "We stormed in and killed all the men first. A lot of guys raped the women and children, and then killed them too. We stole everything in sight and then burned the town down."

I was flabbergasted at the story he just told. I've seen movies about war, but I've never discussed a man's mistakes while he was in war. It didn't matter to me what heinous things he actually did while fighting for our country. That was between him and God. I tried to think of some Scripture to share with him. I told him that all have sinned and come short of the glory of God. I told him the Bible says there's none righteous no not one. We talked briefly about the Ten Commandments. I explained if you've broken one law than you've broken them all. I tried to get him to understand that no one's perfect, and that's why we all need a Savior. We then talked about Jesus and why He went to the cross; to die for the sins of the world. I told him a story of a man named Saul and how he persecuted and killed many Christians before Jesus spoke to him and changed his heart. He became Paul and was a great apostle for Christ and wrote many books of the New Testament.

After discussing the Bible and God's Word I could tell he was starting to shut down. "God can't forgive a sinner like me. I've wronged too many people." I looked at him at said, "That's not how it works. God will forgive you if you ask Him to, no matter what you've done. Jesus paid for everyone's sin when He went to the cross and died for us. All you have to do is accept this and repent of your sins. He will forgive you if you ask Him to." I could see in his eyes that I no longer held his attention. I'll never forget what he said as he stormed off, "God will never forgive a ******* idiot like me."

Some people may not ever understand God's plan of salvation. They may never ask God for forgiveness, and therefore stay lost forever. God knows man, and He knows every man's sin. It's in our nature to sin. He has made a way for us to be pardoned of our sins through the shed blood of Jesus Christ. No matter how atrocious the wickedness is, sin can be forgiven by God. There is nothing too big that God can't do, and there is no sin too big that God won't forgive. Jeremiah 32:27 says: *Behold, I am the* L`ORD`*, the God of all flesh: is there any thing too hard for me?* God is the Creator of all things great and small. He is the Sovereign Creator and Lord of the universe. You can be assured that God loves you and will forgive your every sin. *Behold, I stand at the door, and knock.*

27

Doing God's Will

Let your light so shine before men, that they may see your good works, and glorify your Father which is in heaven.
Matthew 5:16

A few weeks before Christmas, I spoke with a woman on the phone about a used car. I asked her to submit a credit application on the internet, because I feared she had less than perfect credit. During the qualification process, there were several red flags that suggested a credit application would be the best route to go for someone that lived so far away. I didn't want her to drive over two hours if she couldn't get approved for credit. She told me that she would go online and submit the application shortly.

Once I received the application, I reviewed it with our finance department. According to the banks requirements, her income was border line. She did have a good credit score so we sent it to the banks for a credit approval. She told me she needed a car to get her family back and forth to the doctor. A few hours later we had an approval sitting in my office, so I made a call to tell her the good news. We only had one car that would work based on the banks approval. We could make the deal work, but it was a very short deal. We were just moving a unit off the lot, but it needed to go. We had this car sitting here for over sixty days. There wasn't anything wrong with the car. Sometimes cars just don't sell right away. It was now truck season, and everyone was looking for a four wheel drive.

    I went over the payments on the phone because she lived so far away. I also told her that we need four hundred dollars down to make this work with our bank's approval. She asked if the car was a full size and a four door, because she had a large family. I told her it was, and I would have it ready for her for when she arrived.

    I had the car cleaned up and I parked it in front of the dealership. They arrived around two and parked their trade in beside the car I had them approved on. A little girl jumped out of their car and ran straight to the new one. I was watching for them through my office window, and quickly walked outside to greet them. I immediately saw why they needed a four door. Four other people rolled out of their trade in and headed to the new car. Just looking at the family, I could tell that they didn't have a lot of money, but I learned a long time ago to never judge anyone when it came to buying a car. Besides, I already had her approved so all she would have to do is like the car and it would be a deal. I greeted everyone and welcomed them to the dealership. The little girl, bless her heart, was in the back seat shouting to her mom that there was so much room; way more than their old car. She was right. The old car was a four door compact car that had four bald tires, dents on every panel, and looked like it had just been through a war. I'm surprised the old car even made it here. Their old jalopy was way past due for the scrap yard.

Anyone could tell that these folks were from the back country. They spoke and dressed like they were from the country. You know, from the deep part of the woods. Dad and grandpa adorned checkered flannel shirts and jeans. They sported long beards, which were made popular by the television show Duck Dynasty. Grandma also dressed in flannel but had no beard, just a few whiskers. The family was quiet and well-mannered. They called me sir the entire time. Mom was clearly the leader and did all the talking. The mom had snuff squashed between her teeth and jawbone. "I need a spit cup if we are going to take a test drive." I scrambled inside and found a red solo cup to take to her. I wasn't going to let a spit cup stand in the way of a test drive.

I already had a dealer tag screwed on the back and instructed them on our test drive route. I knew they were not familiar with this area, and I didn't want them to get lost. There was no way possible for me to squeeze in and go with them. All five piled into the new car and off they went. While they were on a test drive, I remember thinking about the lady with dip in her lip. This was the first time that I ever saw a woman using dip.

When they came back, I could tell they were in love with the car. I was pretty confident this would be a deal, so I had my finance manager write down the banks terms and payments on the deal sheet while they were driving. The mom and dad set down at my desk as I went to find three more chairs, so everyone could be seated together. I asked, "If we can get all terms agreeable, are you ready to take delivery today?" This is a standard question that you asked before you discuss numbers with the customer. She looked up at me and said, "I wouldn't have driven over two hours if I wasn't ready to buy." That was good enough for me. I flipped over the deal sheet and reviewed the numbers with them. "As you can see, it's exactly what we discussed on the phone." She looked puzzled when I was explaining the numbers. She said, "Well, I was hoping you could wave the down payment because I only have two hundred dollars with me." I knew the bank had cut the finance approval and we were lucky to make the deal work. I explained this in a professional manner to the family and told them the down payment is a must. The mom then said something to me that just blew me away. "I was going to buy a Christmas tree and some presents for my daughter with the two hundred dollars. If I give you the money, then she will have no Christmas."

My heart sunk as I peered around the office at the whole family. She then said, "I'm a Christian and wouldn't lie to you for anything. This is our last two hundred dollars until after the first of January when we get our disability check. I guess we will have to head back home." I could hear the despair and sincerity in her voice. I excused myself and made my to the general manager's office.

I explained to him the situation and asked him what to do. He pulled up the deal on his computer. He thought for a second and said. "I want to help them, but my hands are tied. There is nothing that I can do. We aren't making any money on the deal to change the down payment. It is what it is." I couldn't believe he would lose a deal over two hundred dollars, but I understood where he was coming from. I set in his office a bit longer trying to think of anything I could do to make this work, and then it came to me. I told him, "She has two hundred with her. What if we held a check for the other two hundred for a few weeks?" This wasn't something that we typically did, yet we have done it in the past. I tugged on his heart's strings just a little, "It's Christmas time, c'mon let's help them get a car." That was enough to push him over the edge. He finally said that it was ok to hold a check. "Sell the car."

I went over the good news with the family, but the extra two hundred dollars was a big deal to them. I knew their combined monthly income wasn't much, and my heart went out to them. The grandmother said she could do some extra sewing to help out and cover the down payment. She said they needed a dependable car that would get them back and forth to the doctor, so she would help out anyway she could. I knew they didn't have any money and we were asking to take Christmas away from the little girl because the deal required it, but I still had a job to do. "So we have a deal? Give us two hundred dollars today and we will hold a check for the other two hundred until you get paid. There will be forty-five days before you have your first payment due." The mom looked at the little girl and said, "Are you ok with not having a Christmas tree this year?" The girl replied, "Yes mommy." The mom then said, "You won't have anything to open Christmas day, is that ok?" The girl replied, "Yes mommy." The lady turned to me and said, "Mister, we have a deal."

I made my way to the finance department and asked the manager to draw up the papers; we have a deal. On the way back to my office I couldn't help but think of the little girl. I also knew what God was telling me to do. I asked the mom to take a walk with me. We walked down the hallway and I said, "I need you to be honest with me. Were you serious about not having money for the little girl's Christmas? She stopped walking and said, "Yes. She said she understood." The little girl might have been all of six years old. I've heard of people living paycheck to paycheck but that was just sad. "I'm going to fill the car up with gas. I know you have a long drive home." She thanked me as I walked out the door. I was headed to the gas station, but first I made a little stop.

Wal-Mart was just up the hill from our dealership. I couldn't let that little girl go without a Christmas tree and presents. I grew up without a lot and I remember one year my mom couldn't afford a Christmas present for me. I was older than the little girl at the time so I understood that Christmas wasn't about the presents. I didn't care about getting gifts I just wanted to be with family. To me, that was a gift. The memory of my mom crying on Christmas day was hard for me to see. She was upset that she couldn't provide for me. I didn't want the little girl to have the same memory.

I picked out a nice pre-lit tree with white lights on it. As I went to pay for it, I remembered that I had three gift cards in my wallet that had fifty dollars left on them. I put the new tree and the gift cards in the trunk of their new car, and headed to the gas station to fill up their new car.

The customers were finished with financing by the time I made it back to the dealership. We shook hands and they thanked me for helping them get their new car. I smiled and told them to have a safe trip home. The mother said that they still had a few things to get out of the old car, and that I could go ahead inside out of the cold. I shook her hand again, and with one last thank you made my way back inside.

I set down at my desk and watched the mother grab a bag of their belongings from the old car. Just about then, the little girl came galloping inside. She was screaming so loud that no one could understand what she was trying to say. I thought something horrible happened by the way she was whaling. I rushed to the front of the dealership to get a better understanding of what was going on. She was so overwhelmed that she started sobbing uncontrollably. About that time her mother came through the door to comfort her. My general manager came over to see what the commotion was all about. The lady said, "Somebody put a Christmas tree in the trunk of the car. That's what she was screaming about. Everything's ok." She then looked at me and whispered, "Thank you." I smiled and nodded back at her. She wiped the tears of joy from her daughter's cheeks as they walked out the door.

 I saw their taillights flash as they were leaving the lot, so I went back to my desk to check emails. I was checking to see if I had any internet inquiries in the last few hours that I might've missed while working with the last customers. All of a sudden I heard my general manager page me to the sales desk. As I walked up there I saw all the sales people standing around the desk. They gave me a standing ovation. My GM shook my hand and said, "That was a class act thing you did for those customers. That little girl will never forget what you did for her and her family. You have a customer for life." The only thing that I heard him say was I did all of these things. I knew it wasn't me but God who brought me to this situation. I corrected him. I told everyone, "Don't give me the glory, it's all God. He was the one that told me to do it. I was just doing His will." All the salesmen had a peculiar look on their faces as I walked back to my desk.

I listened to God when He spoke to me. He told me to help out this family in their time of need, and I did so. I hope God's work somehow got through to the unsaved that I worked with. God let my light shine for His glory. I wanted to make sure they knew that this was God's work, and He got the glory from it. It felt so good to hear the little girl's reaction when she came storming through the doors. That was all I needed.

Sometimes we take things for granted. There are a lot of people in this world that do not have food on the table or a place to stay at night. Then there's some that have been blessed more than enough that don't appreciate it at all. This shows that people do still care enough about each other to help in a time of need. Don't take for granted the things that you have been blessed with from God. I thank Him every day for my blessings.

28

Get Right or Get Left

Watch therefore: for ye know not what hour your Lord doth come. **Matthew 24:42**

The day is rapidly approaching when God the Father will send Jesus Christ for His church. This event is known as the rapture. Those that believe in Christ as Savior will one day be caught up to meet Him in the air. The ones remaining will ultimately face God's judgement as it is poured out on the earth. Simply put, we need to get right or get left. We need to get right with the Lord and believe in Him as our Savior, or get left behind.

Scripture shares with us the facts about "Christ's gathering of "His people" in many different books of the Bible. This is explained in Matthew 24:30-35, which reads: *And then shall appear the sign of the Son of man in heaven: and then shall all the tribes of the earth mourn, and they shall see the Son of man coming in the clouds of heaven with power and great glory. And he shall send his angels with a great sound of a trumpet, and they shall gather together his elect from the four winds, from one end of heaven to the other. Now learn a parable of the fig tree; When his branch is yet tender, and putteth forth leaves, ye know that summer is nigh: So likewise ye, when ye shall see all these things, know that it is near, even at the doors. Verily I say unto you, This generation shall not pass, till all these things be fulfilled. Heaven and earth shall pass away, but my words shall not pass away.*

This might sound like the beginning of a major motion picture, but in fact it's actually the dawning of the Church's eternal future. Jesus will one day return for the Christians that remain on earth. In John 14:3, Jesus made us a promise: *And if I go and prepare a place for you, I will come again, and receive you unto myself; that where I am, [there] ye may be also.* Jesus Christ forewarns us of His return for two reasons: so we will know what our future has in store, but also so we will not waste the present.

Let's now take a look at what, when, and where, the rapture will take place. So <u>what</u> exactly is the rapture? Rapture: (răp'chər) noun. All true believers who are still alive before the end of the world will be taken from the earth by Jesus into Heaven. The English word "rapture" is derived from the Latin verb "Rapere" meaning "to carry off," or "to catch up." The rapture of the church is the next step in Jesus' prophetic timeline.

People have often wondered <u>when</u> Jesus will come for his followers. Matthew 24:36-44 answers this question: *But of that day and hour knoweth no man, no, not the angels of heaven, but my Father only. But as the days of Noah were, so shall also the coming of the Son of man be. For as in the days that were before the flood they were eating and drinking, marrying and giving in marriage, until the day that Noe entered into the ark, And knew not until the flood came, and took them all away; so shall also the coming of the Son of man be. Then shall two be in the field; the one shall be taken, and the other left. Two women shall be grinding at the mill; the one shall be taken, and the other left. Watch therefore: for ye know not what hour your Lord doth come. But know this, that if the goodman of the house had known in what watch the thief would come, he would have watched, and would not have suffered his house to be broken up. Therefore be ye also ready: for in such an hour as ye think not the Son of man cometh.*

All the pieces are now in place for the rapture to happen at any time. <u>Where</u> will the rapture take place? The rapture will take place here on earth. God's chosen elect will one day be lifted up from earth and ascend into Heaven to be with Him. 1 Corinthians 15:51-52 NLT describes the rapture happening in the blink of an eye: *But let me reveal to you a wonderful secret. We will not all die, but we will all be transformed! It will happen in a moment, in the blink of an eye, when the last trumpet is blown. For when the trumpet sounds, those who have died will be raised to live forever. And we who are living will also be transformed.*

There are several versus of Scripture that warn us to be vigilant and ready when the rapture happens. Mark 13:35-36: *Watch ye therefore: for ye know not when the master of the house cometh, at even, or at midnight, or at the cockcrowing, or in the morning: Lest coming suddenly he find you sleeping.* Luke 21:34-36 reads: *And take heed to yourselves, lest at any time your hearts be overcharged with surfeiting, and drunkenness, and cares of this life, and so that day come upon you unawares. For as a snare shall it come on all them that dwell on the face of the whole earth. Watch ye therefore, and pray always, that ye may be accounted worthy to escape all these things that shall come to pass, and to stand before the Son of man.*

God provides us the comfort of our friends and family members who die in the Lord. We are told in 1 Corinthians 15:23 that there is an order to this resurrection: Christ was raised as the first of the harvest; then all who belong to Christ will be raised when he comes back. 1 Thessalonians 4:13-18 reads: *But I would not have you to be ignorant, brethren, concerning them which are asleep, that ye sorrow not, even as others which have no hope. For if we believe that Jesus died and rose again, even so them also which sleep in Jesus will God bring with him. For this we say unto you by the word of the Lord, that we which are alive and remain unto the coming of the Lord shall not prevent them which are asleep. For the Lord himself shall descend from heaven with a shout, with the voice of the archangel, and with the trump of God: and the dead in Christ shall rise first: Then we which are alive and remain shall be caught up together with them in the clouds, to meet the Lord in the air: and so shall we ever be with the Lord. Wherefore comfort one another with these words.* Our old bodies, the ones we die in, are corrupted by sin; they cannot enter into the kingdom of Heaven. When we are resurrected by Christ, we will have new bodies, perfect and righteous.

The rapture of the church is when God will call His people home; soon after the tribulation period starts. This is a time when the antichrist merges onto the scene. This time of great distress occurs just prior to Satan being bound and Christ's thousand year reign on earth. During the tribulation period, the wrath of God is poured out on a world that has rejected Him for so long. According to Scripture, the church will be raptured before the tribulation period. The church will already be taken out of this world and will not have to endure God's wrath to come.

How do I prepare for the rapture? We should confess our sins to God and repent, then trust in Jesus Christ as our Lord. We should also spread the good news. I work with people every day that are not saved. Jesus said in Mark 16:15 to go into all the world and preach the Gospel to every creature. We need to get the Gospel out to all the unsaved. Do not take for granted every day that we have, for the Lord could come without a moment's notice. The Book of Revelation 22:12: *And, behold, I come quickly; and my reward is with me, to give every man according as his work shall be.* We should always be looking towards the Heavens for His glorious appearance. Acts 1:11 tells us that we will see Jesus returning in the clouds: *Which also said, Ye men of Galilee, why stand ye gazing up into heaven? this same Jesus, which is taken up from you into heaven, shall so come in like manner as ye have seen him go into heaven.*

Friends, do not heed this warning. You must get right with the Lord or you will be left behind. You do not want to face God's wrath of judgement during the tribulation period. The Bible warns us to be ready and receive Christ; because He's coming fast. Prepare and accept the Lord, because He could come back today. Matthew 25:13 reads: *Watch therefore, for ye know neither the day nor the hour wherein the Son of man cometh.*

Lastly, Christians should not fear the rapture. Your security is in God's Word. Trust that He will take care of you. Remember that God loves us, and is always in control. Matthew 24:27 is God's promise to you: *For as the lightning cometh out of the east, and shineth even unto the west; so shall also the coming of the Son of man be.*

29

Do Not Be a Charlatan

It's good for children to have an imagination. I remember playing cowboys and Indians when I was a kid. The cowboys would put on their ten gallon hat, lone ranger mask, and have their pistol cap gun by their side. They would yell yea-hah and fire their cap guns in the air. The Indians would dress with feathers in their headband, and war paint on their face. They would make homemade bow and arrows with some string and a stick. Indian battle cries and cowboy heartaches echoed the neighborhood. We always had fun pretending. As we grow into adults, we have to put the pretending aside, especially when it comes to God.

Every church has people that do not yet believe. Some are heading in the direction of belief, while others are simply pretenders. These imposters go on living a lie and sadly will never know Jesus as Lord. Just because you go to church doesn't mean you are saved. Jesus said in Matthew 7:22-23: *Many will say to me in that day, Lord, Lord, have we not prophesied in thy name? and in thy name have cast out devils? and in thy name done many wonderful works? And then will I profess unto them, I never knew you: depart from me, ye that work iniquity.*

Jesus said, *Ye shall know them by their fruits.* I worked with a girl who claimed her boyfriend was saved, but his actions proved otherwise. He was an out of work drunk, smoked marijuana, and did many other things that would make you think he was unchristian. 1 John 4:1 NLT says: *Dear friends, do not believe everyone who claims to speak by the Spirit. You must test them to see if the spirit they have comes from God. For there are many false prophets in the world.*

If this man was truly a Christian, then why was he doing all these bad things? 1 Corinthains 6:19 says that the body is a temple of the Holy Spirit. Why would someone want to abuse it with drugs, alcohol, and other unclean things? The Bible teaches us in Matthew 7:16 NLT: *You can identify them by their fruit, that is, by the way they act. Can you pick grapes from thornbushes, or figs from thistles?* Take note: Our witness is at jeopardy anytime a Christian acts out in front of the unsaved. A true believer would repent of these wrongdoings, no matter the circumstance. The Holy Spirit, who indwells inside every believer of Christ, convicts us of all our offenses.

I know people can sometimes make mistakes in life. Believe me, I've made a few big ones. I also know that the devil has a major influence in today's society, and you can easily be persuaded to sin. When life beats you down, that is no reason to give into temptation. If this man is or isn't saved; that is between him and God. The Bible clearly says in Matthew 7:1: Judge not, that ye be not judged. My point is this: When I rededicated my life to Christ in 2007; God changed me. When I confessed my sins and recommitted, He gave me a new heart. I didn't want all the worldly things that I once lusted after. He washed my sins away and cleaned me up. I now have the Holy Spirit who lives inside of me; to convict me if I even think about those old ways. You must turn away from your sins. Jesus repeatedly told people go and sin no more. If you repent of your sins, God will give you a change of heart. We need to be thinking of ways to support each other, especially in times of trials and troubles. The Bible tells us this in Hebrews 10:24: *Let us think of ways to motivate one another to acts of love and good works.*

Paul said that it is up to every man to work out his own salvation. No one will force you to accept God. He works inside of us to give us the will to do what needs to be done to bring about our salvation. We do not serve a presumptuous God. He will never make us accept Him. God has given all of us the free will to choose.

Many people do not understand the full meaning of salvation. They miss out on accepting Him, knowing Him as Savior, and receiving the rewards He has planned for us. I hear a lot of people say that they believe there is a God and that Jesus Christ is his Son. This person usually continues on to say that they are saved because they believe there is a God. People need to be careful not to trust in beliefs of false misunderstandings. Here's an interesting tidbit: Did you know that the devil and his demons also believe there is a God? In fact, they were once in Heaven with God until Satan and his angels tried to overthrow Him and were cast out of Heaven. Their belief that there is a God doesn't make the devil or his demons saved. Just because you believe there is a God, doesn't make you saved either. In Romans 10:9-10 the Bible teaches us the correct way to be saved: *That if thou shalt confess with thy mouth the Lord Jesus, and shalt believe in thine heart that God hath raised him from the dead, thou shalt be saved. For with the heart man believeth unto righteousness; and with the mouth confession is made unto salvation.*

    Here are some common questions that the saved and unsaved alike sometimes struggle with. "When I turn away from my sin, will I ever be tempted again?" Yes. "Will I ever sin again?" Yes. "Will I be perfect after I am saved?" No. "Will God forgive us of our sins?" Yes. We should strive to be like Christ; perfect. God knows our hearts. He also knows we are human and will sin again. That's why He gave us the perfect plan of salvation, so that we will not be separated from Him.

    Jesus is our court appointed advocate before the throne of God. Romans 8:34 says: *Who is he that condemneth? It is Christ that died, yea rather, that is risen again, who is even at the right hand of God, who also maketh intercession for us.* Jesus is our defense attorney. When the prosecutor (Satan) comes before the Lord, he explains to God why you should go to Hell. "He doesn't love you. If he did, this man would not have committed all these horrible sins against you. I move that you sentence him to an eternity of persecution." Our great attorney (Jesus Christ) steps in and pleads our case to the Father. "He committed those sins I agree, but I already paid the price for all of his sins. He is one of mine and the court must let him go." The Judge (God) slams the hammer down and says, "The penalty for him has already been paid in full, case dismissed."

    <u>It's time to give yourself a checkup:</u>

    How do I know that I am truly saved? This is a question a lot of people have from time to time. If you claim that you are saved, but your heart hasn't changed, then you'd better reevaluate yourself. If you do not have the Holy Spirit convicting you of your sins; once again you'd better reexamine yourself. If this describes you then something is not right with your relationship with God. Do not be a charlatan. Pray to Him and God will give you the answers you are seeking.

Don't be the example that Jesus is talking about when He said: <u>Depart from me, I never knew you.</u> Not only will you be forever separated from Him, but you are cheating yourself here on earth by not knowing Him as Lord. Jesus will make your life complete and whole once you accept Him as Savior. I promise you that a relationship with Jesus Christ will change your heart and your life forever.

30

Listening to God

My sheep hear my voice, and I know them, and they follow me. **John 10:27 NLT**

God talks to me; that's right, and I listen. I'm sure this statement may sound crazy to someone who doesn't believe, but it is very true. Sometimes God directs me to say or do something, and other times He just shows me that He loves me. I was speaking to a brother in Christ the other day, and he said, "God never speaks to me." I turned to him and said, "Maybe He does, but do you take the time to listen to Him?" God speaks to us in many ways, not just in our conscience.

Most believers have a prayer relationship with God. This is a great way to communicate with Him. So many times however, the communication can be a one way street if we do not take the time to listen to God. So how does one communicate with God? In this chapter I would like to discuss how God does in fact speak to the believer.

Do you take the time to listen when God speaks to you? With all the hustle and bustle of today's times, it can be easy to neglect God when He calls out to you. We need to take time out of our day to commune with Him. When we talk with Him through prayer we also need to stop and listen. If the Sovereign Creator of the universe speaks to us, we need to listen up and give Him our undivided attention.

We need to speak with God in order to constantly strengthen our relationship with Him. Christians should also talk to Him to seek advice, guidance, wisdom, and about our desires. The believer should have Him in their thoughts throughout the day. We should share what's on our heart with God; the good and the bad. He already knows all our troubles and disharmonies, still He wants us to commune with Him about it. The Lord wants to be involved in every part of our lives, and we should include Him in our decisions. Talking to God shows that we have knowledge and faith in Him for every decision. Let's humble ourselves, kneel down, and call out to God. Open your heart to a most loving and deserving God.

Most of us are comfortable talking to God, but how do you listen when He speaks? Listening to God is one of the most important things we can do. Our future depends on it. Since God is a Spirit, we might need to listen to Him differently than we would a human being. Here are several different ways in which we can hear God speak to us:

He can speak to us through visions and dreams.

Through His written Word in the Bible.

He can speak to us in our prayers.

Divine circumstances.
He can put thoughts into our minds at any time.
He can speak to our conscience by the Holy Spirit.
Through other believers.

One day while I was on my way home from work, God spoke to me. He asked me to witness to a woman that I'd spoken to earlier that day. At first I was hesitant, I was still very young spiritually and feared that I would fail Him. I told Him my thoughts, but the answer was still the same. "Talk to her." I rustled with these thoughts for a few moments and then I finally gave in. I decided that God put this on my heart, so I knew I should obey Him.

Early on the next day, I received a surprise phone call from the lady. She said that she wanted to purchase the vehicle we discussed the previous day, and that she would be in today to pick it up. I couldn't believe what just happened. It wasn't that she wanted to buy the car that took me by surprise; it was the fact that God was working to bring us back together so I could witness to her.

I had the car cleaned and ready to go when she arrived. She set at my desk and I let the finance department know she was here. As soon as we set down to talk, the finance department paged us. I immediately thought the devil was trying to intervene as I walked with her to the finance department.

I'm normally cool, calm, and collected when it comes to talking with a customer, but this time I was a very nervous. I was so nervous that I was shaking from head to toe. A million thoughts raced through my mind. How was I going to start this conversation? What was I going to say? I felt in my heart that I needed to guide conversation towards Jesus, but how would I achieve this? All these thoughts ran through my head as I set at my desk waiting for her return.

I knew this was going to be a challenge for me, so I had in place a scape goat. I normally fill up the customer's car with gas, while they're in finance, but this time I didn't. I didn't want her to shake my hand and get into her car like many other customers do. Too many times customers are excited about driving off in their new cars, they forget to even say goodbye to the salesman. I didn't want that to be the case.

She finished signing her paperwork and was walking to her new car when I caught up to her. I could see she was in a hurry. She told me she needed to get home to her sick husband and started to thank me. My guess was right about her wanting to leave so quickly. I told her that I needed to go fill her car up with gas and I would be right back.

My plan was not working out completely how it played out in my mind. I know that God said to speak to her, but when would I know have the time? I knew she would storm off as soon as I got back from the gas station. Then it came to me. I knew what my next step was going to be. I turned to her and said, "How about you go with me to the gas station?" She said ok as she slid into the passenger's side of the car.

The trip to the gas station was filled with awkward silence. My brow was sweating from the stress of opening up the conversation to her. I drove to the gas station, and told her that I would pump the gas and be right back. It felt like my heart was now pounding out of my chest. My nerves were about to get the best of me. I finished pumping the gas and paid the attendant. As I was heading back to the car, I knew it was now or never, and I was not going to let God down.

I climbed back into her newly purchased vehicle, when she asked me if I filled the car up. I told her, "To the brim." Then I said, "Can I ask you a serious question?" She said, "Sure, go ahead." I asked her, "How is your relationship with God?" I didn't know that's all it took to get her talking. As her eyes filled up with tears, she started to pour her heart out to me. "I know that I should go to church more often than I do. In fact, I haven't been in a few years. Everything's been so hard on me since my husband got sick. He is dying of terminal cancer and only has a few months to live. That's why I am buying this car. He wanted to take care of me before he's gone."

I couldn't believe what she was telling me. I had no idea this lady was in so much pain. I started to tell her about Jesus and asked her if either one of them had been saved? She told me that he was saved, and that she thought she was saved. I explained to her that the Bible teaches us that once you are saved you are always saved. She then shared that she was saved when she was ten or eleven years old, but had fallen away from the church for several years now. She said that she let life get in the way of going to church on Sundays. "Taking care of my three kids is a fulltime job. Plus I'm taking care of my husband too."

I could relate to this lady. I let life get in the way of worshipping the Lord too. As we continued to talk I asked her if we could have prayer together. She said yes. I also told her about God's love and shared with her the trials that I recently endured. I explained to her how Jesus Christ died on the cross for our sins, rose again on the third day, and how He is now sitting on the right hand of the Father in Heaven. She told me that she believes this. I explained to her if she's still unsure if she's saved that we can take care of that right now. She told me that she now knows that she is saved and she just needed to have some reassurance about it. Then we prayed.

After our prayer together ended, I realized our conversation was coming to an end. I told her if she ever needed to talk about anything, don't hesitate to call or stop by. She also assured me that she would take her children to church on Sunday. I never heard from her again.

As I now reflect back on this and think, was God teaching me a lesson in being obedient to Him? I knew without a shadow of a doubt, He told me to reach out to this lady, and I wasn't going to let Him down. I didn't know how I was going to do it, but I knew He would help me find a way.

I'm not sure if the conversation we had together helped me or her more. This lady's story and mine were very similar. I just went through a major trial and she was going through one now. We both neglected to put God first, and let other things stand in the way of our fellowship with Him.

This was the first time that I can remember God talking to me. I'm sure there were other times that God reached out to me, and I failed to hear Him. The sin in my life could have been prohibiting me from hearing Him clearly. I've now experienced a personal relationship with God; I listen to Him when He calls out to me. Once you take the time to actually seek God and listen to Him, you too can grow in your relationship with the Father.

31

Peace after the Storm

No, despite all these things, overwhelming victory is ours through Christ, who loved us. **Romans 8:37 NLT**

When we walk through a storm, remember God is faithful. The Lord walks beside us during our distress. He is there with us and will strengthen us in our time of need. Be of good cheer my friend, our trials only last for a little time. While it might not be easy to see the end while we endure our tribulations, God tells us in Romans 8:37 that we will survive our adversities. Habakkuk 3:17-19 tells us that at the end of our trials, God will bring our lives to new heights and strengthen our relationship with Him. I know this to be true; He did it for me. I was broken and God took me, cleaned me up, and set me on the right path to follow Him.

May 23rd 2007 forever changed my life. Although I had to overcome adversity, God delivered me from my affliction and abundantly blessed my family and I. God knew exactly what needed to happen to me before I would see the error of my ways and turn back to Him. I once was ignorant and blind, but God gave me the knowledge of His Word, and opened my eyes, so that I can now see the truth.

My accident was truly a blessing from God. My Lord was working behind the scenes before, during, and after my recovery. While I laid still in a coma, my mother called my father to give him the dreadful news. My father and I have been estranged for many years. My accident was the beginning of our relationship, and the healing process that was long overdue. It also sparked and rekindled a love between my mother and father. In August 2008, on his birthday; they were married. My mother was also saved and baptized. She told me that she made a promise to God that if somehow He would spare my life, she would serve Him faithfully forevermore. This is a promise that I know she will always keep. The only prayer that I really ever prayed before my accident finally came true. My family was together again, thanks to God.

My wife didn't see or understand the blessing that would soon be headed her way. She struggled for many years with which direction she wanted her life to go. She was in a rut with her job, and did not want to be stuck in this position for the rest of her life. As she spent many months by my side, attending to my every need, she helped me walk and talk again. With every step of my recovery, her confidence grew. If God hadn't blessed me with such a great wife, my recovery might have taken much longer. My wife stood beside me in sickness and in health, and went out of her way to care for my needs.

My accident prepared my wife and gave her the strength and determination to become a nurse. We had a conversation one day about it. "Do you think I could do it? Do you think I would be a good nurse?" There wasn't any doubt in my mind she would make a great nurse. Any hospital would be glad to have her.

I supported her decision and she went back to school to become a Registered Nurse. She started by taking a few classes at the college in town. She was then picked to go to nursing school. After a few years of hard work, she graduated with honors. She now works in the Neurology department at a local hospital, treating people with head traumas for a living. Her passion to help others in need, was all part of God's plan.

My accident brought my family much closer together. The strained relationships were now all void, as everyone in my family was there to visit and spend time with me. I am happy to say that I am now 99% back to normal. My thinking is clear and my body is strong. I still struggle with aphasia, where I can't remember the word I want to use to describe something, but I have learned to cope with it. My peripheral vision is still damaged in my left, but it is good enough to pass an eye exam so I can drive. My body will never be the same that is once was, but I am okay with that. My wife tells me I am now more handsome than I was before. I think that's funny every time she says it.

I will never take for granted again the gift of being able to walk. I remember when this was a challenge for me. Walking is such a simple task for most, yet if you ever experience this disability, you would agree. I now participate in local races and enjoy every second of it. The challenge of the course and the thrill of winning has become my new hobby.

The most important thing that happened to me above all, is my relationship is now stronger with my Lord God. I read and listen to his Word daily and meditate in His teachings. I walk and talk with Him every step of the way. I know when He is pleased with me, and when He is not. I know He feels every pain that I suffer and He knows every thought I have of Him. I am a true disciple of Christ and serve only Him. I may sometimes stumble and fall along life's way, but I know my Lord is there to pick me up, dust me off, and put me back on the right path.

The day of my baptism, my pastor and I were having a conversation, and I brought up that I played guitar. I told him that if he'd ever need a guitarist I would play. He asked if I could play the bass guitar. I joyously said yes. I'd missed playing in a band for quite some time, and God answered my prayer. Playing bass guitar is such a blessing to me each Sunday morning. I often thank God for the talent to play. Just being able to play music for

Him warms my heart each Sunday. I thank Him for bringing me to the little church on the hill. This was just another part of God's plan.

Listen friend. I was once blinded. I believed in God, yet lacked the most important thing to being a Christian, and that's a personal relationship with Him. Like so many that are new believers in Christ, I didn't know what my next steps should have been after I accepted Jesus Christ as Savior. No one explained to me how to grow and fellowship as a Christian. I didn't know how to accept God's love and walk with Him. I was blinded and ignorant until God showed me He cared for me. I had to make it through a heavy trial before my eyes were opened and I saw the truth. I realized after twenty-seven years, God is alive, and God loves me.

The Lord wants an intimate relationship with us. He wants to be able to give us love, joy, and happiness. He also wants to receive our love and obedience. A close personal intimate relationship with God through Jesus Christ is the most important thing in our lives.

Once we are saved, we must grow in order to have a relationship with Him. 2 Peter 3:18 tells us: *But grow in grace, and in the knowledge of our Lord and Saviour Jesus Christ. To him be glory both now and for ever. Amen.* The Bible needs to be our roadmap in life. Reading Scripture daily will enable you to grow in wisdom and knowledge, and bring you into a personal relationship with Jesus Christ our Savior.

Jesus promises that He will never leave us or forsake us. That's why the Holy Spirit dwells inside of us, so we can have that personal relationship with Him. He's with us in the good times and in our broken times. My friend, the key to living a fruitful Christian life is having an intimate relationship with Jesus Christ. This I know.

God recently spoke to me and told me to write this book. I was sitting in my living room one day and He spoke to my conscience. He said in a clear voice simply, "Write the book." I setup from my chair and pondered on what I just heard my conscience say. I knew this was the voice of God talking to me. I heard it as clear as day. What did God mean when He told me, "Write the book?" A split second later I knew exactly which book He was referring to as my mind focused wholly on Him. My prayer is that this book will touch someone and lead them to know and trust the Lord, and to have instruction on what to do next once you are saved. It has truly been a blessing for me to write it. Writing this book has brought me closer to Him.

Believe me when I tell you this my friend. When you see a storm brewing on the horizon, turn to the Lord for wisdom and guidance. Proverbs 3:5-6 tells us: *Trust in the LORD with all thine heart; and lean not unto thine own understanding.*

In all thy ways acknowledge him, and he shall direct thy paths. No matter if you are experiencing the smallest storm in life or a massive hurricane, always remember this promise from God: *I know the LORD is always with me. I will not be shaken, for he is right beside me.* Psalms 16:8 NLT

Friend, do not forsake God's offer of salvation. Accept Jesus Christ as Savior before it's too late. Grow in His Word and wisdom, and seek a personal relationship with Him now. This is the best decision that you will ever make in your life, I assure you. Revelation 3:20 says: *Behold, I stand at the door, and knock: if any man hear my voice, and open the door, I will come in to him, and will sup with him, and he with me.* Jesus Christ is knocking at your heart's door, won't you let Him in?

It's been eight years since my accident. In the beginning of my storm, the skies were dark and dreary, with no end in sight. The storm came all of a sudden, without notice. I tried making my way through the storm by myself, but I was lost. I needed someone to help get me through the storms of life. Thankfully, I found my Savior.

Jesus Christ is my lighthouse. If it wasn't for Jesus, where would I be? I've endured some hardships along the way, but by the loving grace of God, I have peace after the storm. God has now showed this disciple of Christ, his purpose in life.

Made in the USA
Charleston, SC
04 January 2016